Self-Discovery

One of the five books in the *Mental Health and Wellbeing* resource focuses on how to support children and young people in Self-Discovery, as they learn to be their own best friend. The book offers research-driven, practical strategies, along with creative material and step-by-step lesson plans to support educators and health professionals. This is a resource book for practitioners looking to have a positive impact on the mental health and wellbeing of the children and young people in their care; both now and in the future.

Chapters span key topics including Developing Resilience, Positive Thinking, Emotional Awareness and Self-Efficacy. A complete toolkit for teachers and counsellors, this book offers:

- Easy to follow, and flexible, lesson plans that can be adapted and personalised for use in lessons or smaller groups or 1:1 work

- Resources that are linked to the PSHE and Wellbeing curriculum for KS1, KS2 and KS3

- New research, 'Circles for Learning', where the introduction of baby observation into the classroom by a teacher is used to understand and develop self-awareness, skills for learning, relationships, neuroscience and awareness of others

- Sections on the development of key skills in communication, skills for learning, collaboration, empathy and self-confidence

- Learning links, learning objectives and reflection questions.

Offering research-driven, practical strategies and lesson plans, *Self-Discovery* is an essential resource book for educators and health professionals looking for fresh, engaging ways to support the wellbeing of children and young people.

Alison Waterhouse has worked in mainstream, special education and the independent sector for the past 30 years, specialising in working with children with AEN including Mental Health and Wellbeing. She has set up and developed an Independent Therapeutic Special School; and developed a role as Teacher in Charge of the Social and Emotional Wellbeing of the Whole School Community, has been an Inclusion Manager and Deputy Head in mainstream Schools. She now works as an Independent Educational Consultant for SEN and Wellbeing, is involved in staff training; and has her own Educational Psychotherapy practice. Alison works with children who are referred due to difficulties with self-esteem, anger, anxiety, depression and other Mental Health needs as well as children with learning differences. Alison is developing the Circles for Learning Project in schools and has already undertaken a Primary Research Project and is now working on a Secondary Research Project. The resources were put together to support staff with these projects.

The invisible roots of learning

- Emotional literacy
- Self-discovery
- Skills for effective learning in school
- Positive relationships in school
- The brain and learning

Self-Discovery
Supporting Emotional Health and Wellbeing in School

Alison Waterhouse

Routledge
Taylor & Francis Group
LONDON AND NEW YORK

First published 2019
by Routledge
2 Park Square, Milton Park, Abingdon, Oxon OX14 4RN

and by Routledge
52 Vanderbilt Avenue, New York, NY 10017

Routledge is an imprint of the Taylor & Francis Group, an informa business

© 2019 Alison Waterhouse

The right of Alison Waterhouse to be identified as author of this work has been asserted by her in accordance with sections 77 and 78 of the Copyright, Designs and Patents Act 1988.

All rights reserved. The purchase of this copyright material confers the right on the purchasing institution to photocopy pages which bear the photocopy icon and copyright line at the bottom of the page. No other parts of this book may be reprinted or reproduced or utilised in any form or by any electronic, mechanical, or other means, now known or hereafter invented, including photocopying and recording, or in any information storage or retrieval system, without permission in writing from the publishers.

Trademark notice: Product or corporate names may be trademarks or registered trademarks, and are used only for identification and explanation without intent to infringe.

British Library Cataloguing-in-Publication Data
A catalogue record for this book is available from the British Library

Library of Congress Cataloging-in-Publication Data
A catalog record for this book has been requested

ISBN: 978-1-138-37025-8 (pbk)
ISBN: 978-0-429-42811-1 (ebk)

Typeset in Avant Garde
by Apex CoVantage, LLC

Printed by Ashford Colour Press Ltd.

To Dave, for turning on the lights and showing me the many options available at a very dark time. I am eternally grateful.

Contents

	Introduction	xi
CHAPTER 1	Developing resilience	1
	What is resilience? Our 'bounce back' ability	3
	My gifts and qualities box	7
	Persistence and resilience	10
	My resilience tree	15
	Resilience snakes and ladders	19
CHAPTER 2	Problem solving	23
	Problem solving 1	25
	Problem solving 2	29
	Organisation	33
	Asking for and accepting help from other people	39
CHAPTER 3	Emotional reactivity	43
	Developing the art of gratitude	45
	Thoughts, Feelings, Actions Triangle: Self-limiting beliefs	51
	Thoughts, Feelings, Actions Triangle: Thinking errors	57
	My comfort zone	61
CHAPTER 4	Positive thinking	67
	Developing positive self-talk	69
	Think of it in another way: Reframing	72

Contents

	The best mistake I ever made!	80
	Rose-tinted glasses	83
	There is only one person responsible for your happiness	87
CHAPTER 5	Emotional awareness and self-regulation	91
	Self-regulation	93
	Stress management techniques	97
	The anxiety hit squad!	102
	Threat or reward	105
	Making mind movies	109
	Let's relax	113
	Being brave, having courage	116
	Creative meditation or stress busting for dummies!	119
	My incredible talking body	123
CHAPTER 6	Empathy	127
	Walking in another person's shoes 1	129
	Walking in another person's shoes 2	132
	Mirror neurons	135
	Different points of view	138
CHAPTER 7	Self-efficacy and responsibility	143
	Self-esteem: What we believe about ourselves	145
	Only one of you	151
	Self-esteem, self-limiting beliefs	155
	My 'I did it' gallery	162
	People we admire	166

Contents

Get to know your best friend	170
You are your own best friend	174
Be your own life coach	180
Bibliography	185

Introduction

SELF-DISCOVERY

How we see and understand ourselves is a personal construction created by the interactions and experiences we have from an early age. How we think about ourselves impacts on how we interpret the world around us and the interactions we have.

When we are born we have a genetic makeup which influences our biological traits. However, who we are develops over time and is very much influenced by our social interactions with others. Many researchers in the fields of psychology and sociology have described the process of self-development.

It is the child's interpretation of life experiences which determines self-esteem levels. It is not the events which a child experiences, as such, that determine emotions but the interpretation of those events. The foundations for self-esteem are laid early in a child's life when they develop attachments with a caring responsive adult who is attuned to them. Several developmental psychologists have emphasised the role of early affective experiences in determining an individual's sense of self-worth. This sense of self-worth is likely to be the foundation of self-esteem.

If there is a mismatch between how a child sees themselves (self-image) and how they would like to be (ideal self) then this affects how much they like or value themselves. This self-esteem impacts on how they then interact with and interpret the world in which they live.

Research has shown that self-esteem is an important psychological factor that contributes to our mental health and wellbeing and it has been shown to be the most dominant and powerful factor in happiness.

Research strongly suggests that teachers can influence a child's self-esteem because attitudes about oneself are more easily influenced if the person who sets out to change attitudes has a high status and is capable of making positive relationships with the child.

The role of self-esteem in adolescent development is well documented, with evidence showing that low self-esteem is associated with depression, suicide, delinquency and substance misuse. Researchers have found correlations between self-esteem and academic success, low anxiety and robust mental health. Studies have also shown that self-esteem increases as a natural

Introduction

outcome of successful life adjustment rather than its root cause. In school, when students do well, self-esteem grows; it follows but does not precede the academic success.

Self-esteem has its taproot in the experience of efficacy. Self-efficacy is not built on what others do or what the environment provides but is based on what one can make the environment provide, even if it is only through infants' more vigorous sucking or louder cries that last for longer. The feeling of efficacy is regulated by the success or failures of infants' efforts, as they have no understanding of what else may be contributing to their failures or successes. From this standpoint, self-esteem has to be closely linked to feelings of efficacy as it develops, and the general cumulative sense of competence.

Self-efficacy beliefs determine how people think, feel, motivate themselves and behave. Such beliefs produce these different effects through 4 main processes: cognitive; motivational; affective; and selection. A strong sense of self-efficacy or self-confidence enables self-accomplishment and therefore has an impact on wellbeing in many ways. People with strong self-confidence take on tasks with a belief that they are challenges which can be achieved. They argue that failure is due to insufficient effort or a lack of knowledge or skills and not due to themselves. This way of looking at things reduces stress and lowers vulnerability to depression. For those with a low sense of self-confidence, the challenge is perceived as a threat to be avoided. They dwell on their lack of skills and personal deficiencies, the obstacles they might encounter, and so become stressed and fall into depression.

Self-awareness is the psychological state in which people become aware of their traits, feelings and their behaviour. It is the ability to try and understand who we really are and why we respond and do the things that we do. If we are aware of ourselves and how we think, respond and behave then this self-knowledge gives us the opportunity to change things. By being self-aware, we gain an increased degree of control over how we operate.

Self-awareness is a core component of emotional intelligence. If we can be aware of our thinking and how this impacts on our behaviours, then we can start to challenge our thoughts and our actions. The more we know about ourselves, the better we become at making changes or adapting to life's challenges.

Our mindset is what we think, and how we manipulate this to fit into our beliefs and values framework. This is an area that is linked to self-awareness and has been developed enormously in recent years by the work of Carol Dweck. Dweck (2007) stated that children and young people have either a fixed or a growth mindset and that these mindsets create frameworks for interpreting and responding to the events that they experienced. If people have a fixed mindset, then they believe that intelligence is static and that because of this some people are smart and some are not. If people have a growth mindset, then they believe that intelligence can be

Introduction

developed by effort or instruction. Mindsets do not imply that everyone is the same, but what they do imply is that everyone's intellectual ability can grow.

Once we become self-aware of our thoughts feelings and behaviours, it takes us one step closer to learning how to regulate and manage them. Developing the ability to regulate our thoughts emotions and attention is a crucial part of childhood development.

Susan Calkins (1994) has described the pathways of emotional regulation as both internal and external. Internal mechanisms are those of the neuroregulatory structures, behaviour traits and cognitive traits and external features are care giving patterns, responsiveness, co-operation and reciprocity.

Terms such as self-control, impulse control and willpower have all been used a great deal in work focusing on human development. Professor Walter Mischel's marshmallow test (1960) explored the delayed gratification development in children. Mischel showed that self-control is not only about making sensible choices but that it is also about capacity to sustain goal-directed action over time. He found that some children were able to delay gratification and therefore researchers established self-control as a personal trait. The research on self-control has shown that it is more important than IQ in predicting successful outcomes for children and young people (Mischel 2015).

The work of Dr Stuart Shanker has extended the field of self-regulation (Shanker 2016). He has shown that, the more stress a child is under, the more difficult their brain finds it to regulate. Chronic states of hyperarousal make the limbic alarm so sensitive to stress that it takes very little to set it off. Perception itself becomes primed to look for threats, which makes perfect evolutionary sense. Scientists have shown that increasing the stress on subjects depletes their self-control and ability to regulate themselves. Learning how to calm and regulate as well as how to access our learning zone can support both learning within the classroom and self-development, both of which impact on our mental health and wellbeing.

Introduction

THE CIRCLES FOR LEARNING PROJECT

Circles for Learning is a unique research-based, whole class or small group project that builds the positive foundations for Mental Health and Wellbeing. It supports and strengthens learning skills alongside the development of social skills, emotional literacy and wellbeing. It facilitates and encourages children to experience how learning happens and explore brain development, relationships and emotions. This includes how other people might feel or experience situations, how to manage emotions, discover our sense of self and understand how our beliefs influence our behaviour.

Circles for Learning has been developed by Alison Waterhouse over the past five years. Alison initiated the Circles for Learning Project in primary schools in East Sussex, where she led and developed this innovative way of working with children. As colleagues became aware of her work, they asked to get involved, so Alison set up the Primary Research Project for five schools in East Sussex where she worked closely with the class teachers to both design and develop the project in their schools. This enabled her to work in both small rural schools and very deprived large urban schools as well as with a variety of teachers. As a result of the interest of professionals in the Secondary field, Alison has just completed a research project with 4 different secondary schools to explore and measure the impact of the work within their environment. This work has been the core of a research MA in Education with the University of York.

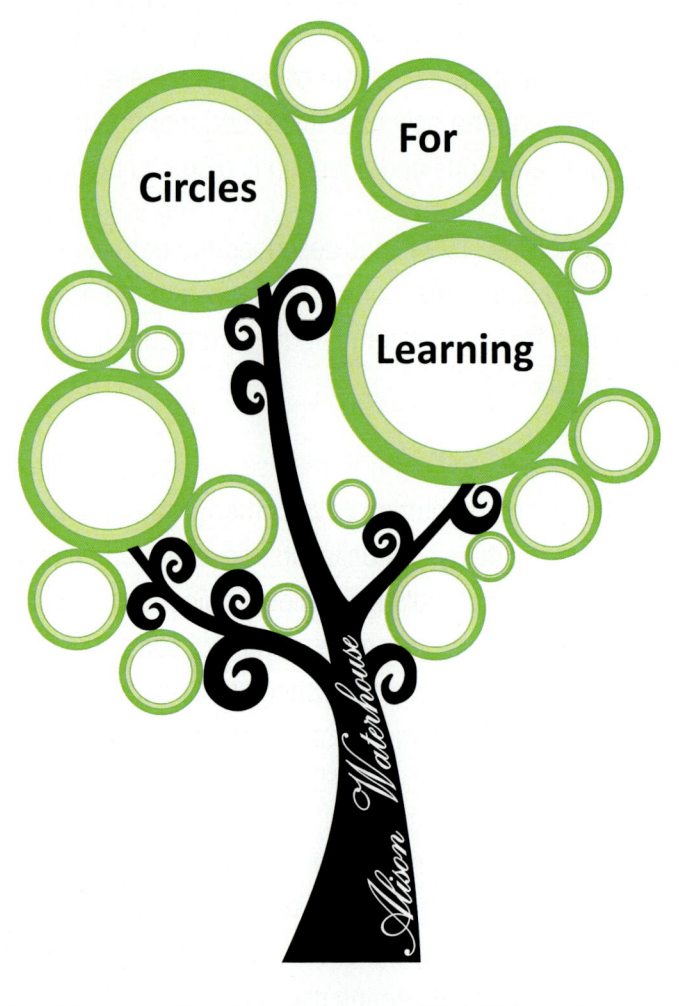

Introduction

The project trains and then supports teachers to bring a parent and baby into the classroom once a month for a year. The children and young people are supported in observing the interactions, learning, relationships and the baby's early developing sense of self. Then, with the support of the teacher, they explore and think about what they have seen and how this may link to their own development, thinking, behaviour and ways of interacting with others.

These observations are the provocation or stimulus to follow-up work led by the teacher exploring one of the Circles for Learning's five areas of work:

1. Emotional competencies: including recognising emotions, managing our own emotions, recognising emotions in others and developing strategies to cope and deal with these emotions.

2. Relationships: including social skills, the learning relationship, social inclusion and empathy.

3. Self-discovery: including self-concept, self-esteem, self-efficacy, self-regulation, self-talk, self-compassion, mindsets and resilience.

4. Skills for effective learning.

5. Neuroscience and learning.

These five key areas form the foundations for Mental Health and Wellbeing. The follow-up work is not a scheme of work to be followed regardless of the needs of the children and young

Introduction

people but a wide range of activities that the teacher can refer to and use that supports the needs of the group at that time.

The resources within each of the five books in the *Mental Health and Wellbeing Toolkit* can be used as standalone resources to support the five key areas that create the foundations for Mental Health and Wellbeing or as part of the Circles for Learning Project.

Introduction

TRACKING SHEET

NAME/GROUP:	
DATE:	**TERM:**
ASSESSMENTS UNDERTAKEN:	**OTHER INFORMATION:**
Date	Lesson:	Comments
Date	Lesson:	Comments
Date	Lesson:	Comments
Date	Lesson:	Comments
Date	Lesson:	Comments
Date	Lesson:	Comments
Date	Lesson:	Comments
Date	Lesson:	Comments
Date	Lesson:	Comments
Date	Lesson:	Comments

Introduction

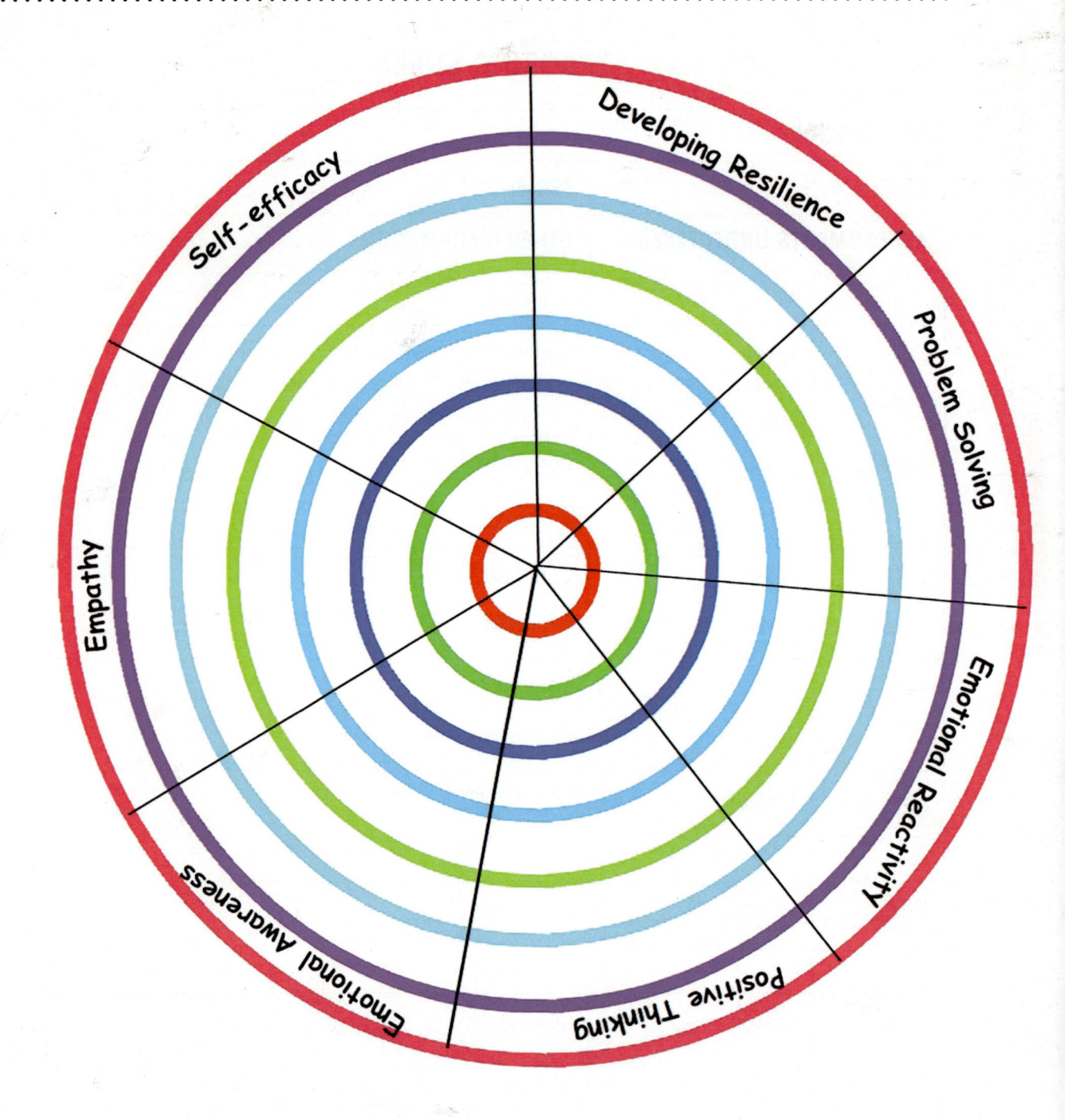

(Circular tracking diagram with eight segments labelled: Self-efficacy, Developing Resilience, Problem Solving, Emotional Reactivity, Positive Thinking, Emotional Awareness, Empathy, and one unlabelled segment.)

The circular tracking document has been designed to allow practitioners to monitor and track the areas that they have covered with the children. As each lesson is covered they are entered onto the document within the focus section. This enables practitioners to see the particular focus they are taking with their group. For some classes they may present a high need within a particular area or a strength in another area and so this can be shown and monitored. The document also allows for other lessons/activities to be added to the document that may have extended knowledge and understanding in this area from PSHE or Circle Time focus.

The document allows the flexibility to meet the needs of the children as they arise rather than having to follow a pre-set curriculum and in so doing allows practitioners to clearly see the areas of need and what they are doing to meet them.

Chapter 1
Developing resilience

WHAT IS RESILIENCE? OUR
'BOUNCE BACK' ABILITY 3

MY GIFTS AND QUALITIES BOX 7

PERSISTENCE AND RESILIENCE 10

MY RESILIENCE TREE 15

RESILIENCE SNAKES AND
LADDERS 19

Developing resilience

What is resilience? Our `bounce back' ability

SESSION OBJECTIVES

To understand what resilience is and how we can strengthen it within ourselves.

SESSION OUTCOMES

- ✓ To create a poster/bookmark/animated video clip to remind us how important it is to develop our resilience and not give up.

LESSON PLAN

- ➢ Remind the children of a time when their class baby was finding things difficult. Discuss what they did, how they reacted and what the parent did, and how they responded.

- ➢ Remind them about how they felt when they saw the baby struggle and what they wanted to do – was this what the baby needed? How would they know?

- ➢ Share video clip.

For those classrooms not able to undertake the Circles for Learning Project, video clips or photographs can be used to support the discussion around the topic and stimulate thoughts and ideas from the children and young people.

1. Show the children a ball of modelling clay and tennis ball and ask what will happen if you drop them both.

Developing resilience

2. Demonstrate and highlight how the modelling clay has got stuck and gone nowhere but the ball has bounced back ready to try again.

3. Explain that this is what resilience is – our 'bounce back' factor.

4. Ask the children/young people to think of a time when they found something really hard and gave up and walked away. How did they feel?

5. Ask them to think of a time when they found something really hard but kept going. – What kept them going? Was it:– someone helping them, positive self-talk, the fact that there was a good reason?

6. How did they feel when they succeeded?

7. Discuss the different strategies that they have described and record them on the board. Ask them to choose which one they might try next time that they haven't tried before and why.

8. Record this as a class list – so you can check in on how they are doing in the future.

Task

Poster KS1
Bookmark KS2/3
Video animation KS3

Poster

Discuss what a poster must share with people and identify the success criteria of a good poster.

- Eye-catching

- Colourful

- Catchphrase

Ask the children to draw/use a photograph of themselves/find a photograph, that shows themselves or someone else being resilient.

Ask the children to find or create a catchphrase to go with this and then create a poster to show what resilience is and to help people develop resilience.

Bookmark

Ask the children to think about why a bookmark could help them develop their resilience. Recap on the strategies they came up with in part 1.

Developing resilience

Identify the success criteria for a good bookmark.

- Size

- Clear

- Catchphrase

- Easy to understand

Ask the children to make a bookmark to remind them about resilience and strategies to use to help them bounce back.

Video animation

Ask the children to think about what makes a good animation.

Recap on the strategies to develop resilience that they identified in part 1.

Identify success criteria for a good animation about resilience.

- Clear

- Easily understood

- Short and to the point

When the children have completed their task, ask them to share or create a mini exhibition where they can share their creation. Ask them to share the ups and downs of creation and the process they had to go through.

Link how they respond to frustration and not being able to achieve something with the baby. Link how you as the teacher feel to the way the parent responded i.e. how you have to respond in 30 different ways!!

RESOURCES

1. Pens for flip chart

2. Sticky notes

3. Paper and pens

4. Coloured pens

5. Card

Developing resilience

6. Laminator

7. Sticky stars etc.

IMPORTANT POINTS

- That resilience can be strengthened and developed with practice.
- That we can use a range of strategies to help us keep going.

LEARNING LINKS

Speaking and listening, collaboration, information processing, questioning, observation, creativity, planning and organisation, teamwork.

REFLECTION

Questions:

Positive comment from child:

Positive comment from adult:

LEARNING DIMENSIONS		SOCIAL & EMOTIONAL SKILLS	
Strategic awareness	🟧	Emotional literacy	🟩
Learning relationships	🟧	Neuroscience	
Curiosity	🟧	Self-regulation	
Creativity	🟧	Self-development	🟩
Meaning making	🟧		
Changing & learning	🟩		
Resilience	🟩		

Developing resilience

My gifts and qualities box

SESSION OBJECTIVES

To be able to identify and celebrate our gifts and qualities.

To be able to celebrate the uniqueness of each individual.

SESSION OUTCOMES

✓ To create a box containing gifts and qualities about ourselves to celebrate our uniqueness.

LESSON PLAN

➢ To share a picture of the class baby in the classroom. Ask the children to discuss why he/she is so special. What do they enjoy about them coming into class?

For those classrooms not able to undertake the Circles for Learning Project, video clips or photographs can be used to support the discussion around the topic and stimulate thoughts and ideas from the children and young people.

Task

KS1/2: To create a special box that contains gifts and qualities about ourselves to celebrate our uniqueness.
To identify gifts and qualities that we have that we are proud of.

1. To discuss in partners what gifts or talents we believe we have.

2. Share the range of talents and gifts we have and make a class list.

3. Share our 2 best qualities with a partner.

4. Share these with the class and create a qualities list.

5. Ask the children to make a box that they are going to use to put the gifts and qualities they have identified about themselves into.

Developing resilience

OR

Create a label for a jam jar that they can put their gifts and qualities in.

6. On small pieces of paper, write in special writing a gift or quality. Tie it up with a piece of ribbon. Put it in the box or jar.

7. Add to this throughout the term as children learn something new or achieve something new – music lessons, spellings, book bands, badges at Brownies or Guides, sports awards, etc.

8. Share the story *Only One You* by Linda Kranz.

9. Ask the children to choose a pebble – each one is different so this represents that they are all different and special.

10. Decorate the pebble with paints or cut out paper pictures so that it is a unique pebble for a unique child. Add them to the children's box.

11. What would the piece of advice they would give themselves be for the year? Add this to their box.

RESOURCES

1. Sticky notes
2. Box template
3. Paper and pens
4. Ribbon
5. Jam jars

IMPORTANT POINTS

- We are unique and individual people

LEARNING LINKS

Thoughts, feelings, actions, self-talk, own best friend, relaxation.

Developing resilience

REFLECTION

Questions:

Positive comment from child:

Positive comment from adult:

LEARNING DIMENSIONS		SOCIAL & EMOTIONAL SKILLS	
Strategic awareness		Emotional literacy	🟩
Learning relationships	🟧	Neuroscience	
Curiosity	🟧	Self-regulation	
Creativity	🟧	Self-development	🟩
Meaning making	🟧		
Changing & learning	🟩		
Resilience	🟩		

Developing resilience

Persistence and resilience

SESSION OBJECTIVES

To experience and practise what it means to be persistent and resilient. To be able to keep going when things get difficult. To pick yourself up and go again.

SESSION OUTCOMES

- ✓ Strategies for achieving our goals.
- ✓ Understand the importance of persistence and resilience in achieving our goals.

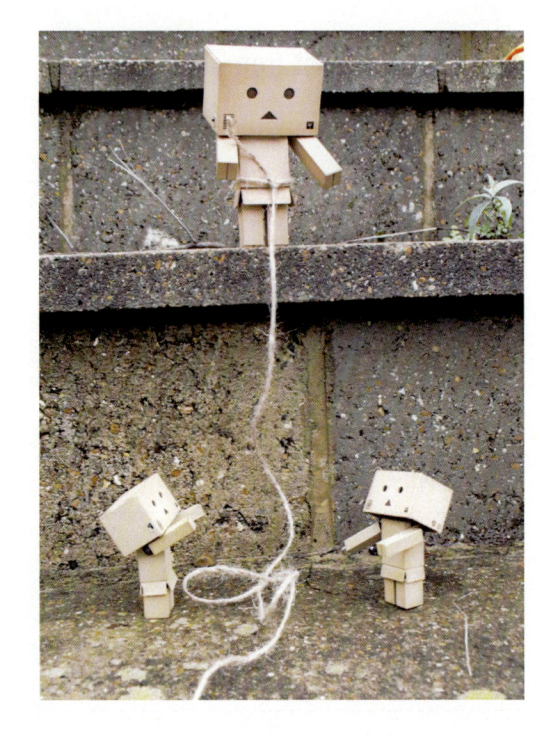

LESSON PLAN

- ➢ Show the video clips of toddlers learning to stand and walk. Link with the observations of your class baby and how they have learnt to do things. Remind the children/young people of how difficult it has been at times.

- ➢ Ask them to identify what allows the toddler to continue.

For those classrooms not able to undertake the Circles for Learning Project, video clips or photographs can be used to support the discussion around the topic and stimulate thoughts and ideas from the children and young people.

Task
KS1: To draw a picture of a dog with their wrong hand and to be coached by a partner.
KS2/3: To draw a picture of a dog with their wrong hand and to be coached by a partner.
   To write a short piece as neatly as possible blindfolded but supported by a partner.

1. In pairs, ask the children/young people to decide who will be the coach and who will be the artist.

2. The artist is asked to draw a dog eating a bone with their wrong hand. The coach must give the artist advice and encouragement to improve their drawing and make them try 2 more times.

Developing resilience

3. Ask the pairs to swap over. What had the coach learnt after being the artist? Did they do things differently?

4. Try a second activity. Blindfold one partner and then ask them to write their name and address/short piece as neatly as they can.

5. Link with things the children/young people have learnt – reading, skateboarding, riding a bike. That they only learn by being persistent – keep going when it gets tough.

6. Get them to think of a time when they have done this.

7. Link with the work already done on being a good coach, your own best friend and self-talk.

8. In pairs write down the top 3 tips for positive coaching. Share these with the class and come up with the class top 10.

Introduce the concept WII4Me (What is in it for me).

RESOURCES

1. Paper

2. Pens

3. Blindfolds

4. WII4ME poster

5. Sticky notes

6. Posters: 'I get knocked down' and 'Genius'

7. Paper and pens

8. Toddlers learning to stand and walk videos:

https://www.youtube.com/watch?v=v06EQgzqvWg (accessed 6 November 2018)

https://www.youtube.com/watch?v=G0oquuOq49I (accessed 6 November 2018)

IMPORTANT POINTS

- Self-talk

- Belief in what we are doing

Developing resilience

LEARNING LINKS

Speaking and listening, collaboration, information processing, questioning, observation, creativity, planning and organisation, teamwork.

REFLECTION

Questions:

Positive comment from child:

Positive comment from adult:

LEARNING DIMENSIONS		SOCIAL & EMOTIONAL SKILLS	
Strategic awareness		Emotional literacy	🟩
Learning relationships	🟧	Neuroscience	
Curiosity	🟧	Self-regulation	
Creativity	🟧	Self-development	🟩
Meaning making	🟧	Resilience	
Changing & learning	🟩		
Resilience	🟩		

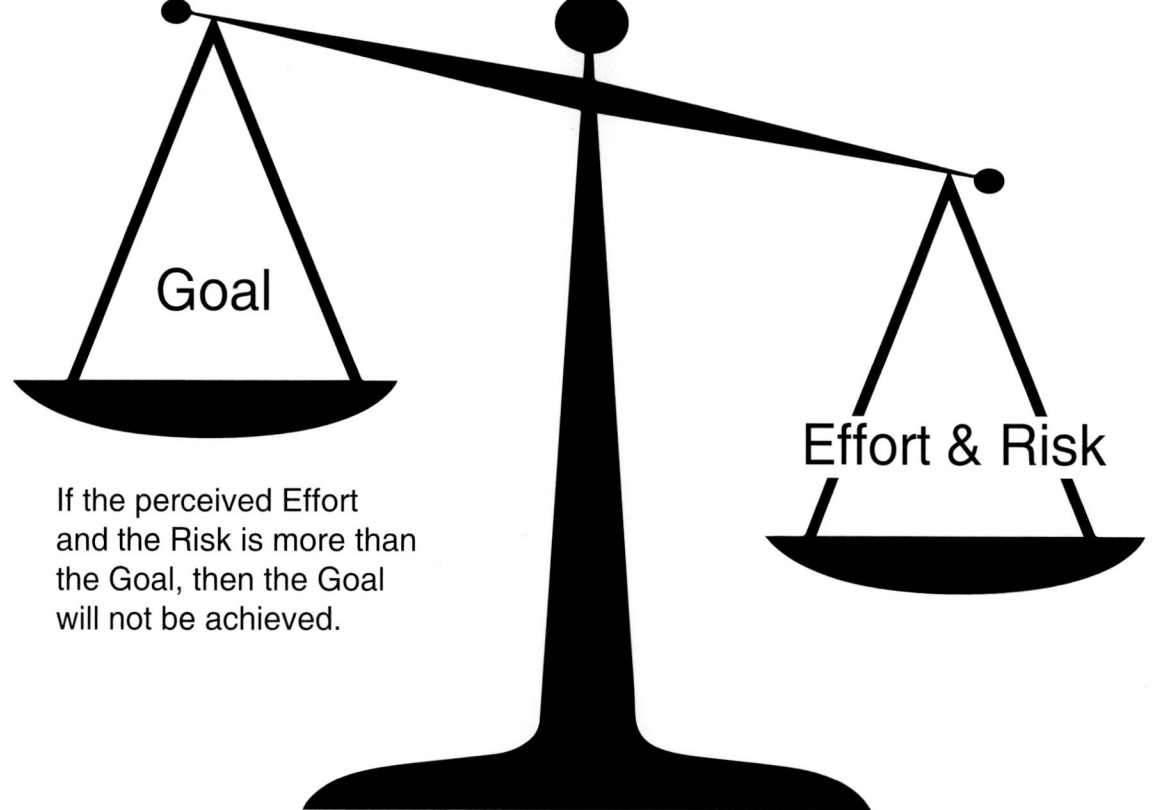

Developing resilience

Effort & Risk

Goal

If the perceived Effort and the Risk is less than the Goal, then the Goal can be achieved.

Goal

Effort & Risk

If the perceived Effort and the Risk is more than the Goal, then the Goal will not be achieved.

Developing resilience

For extra inspiration, please look up Albert Einstein's quote about a fish in a tree

Developing resilience

My resilience tree

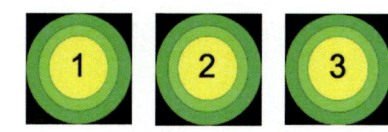

SESSION OBJECTIVES

1. To enable the children to identify their strengths and strategies to meet life's challenges.

2. To enable the children to identify the many areas that they can seek help from if they need to.

SESSION OUTCOMES

✓ To be able to discuss their strengths and strategies to manage life's challenges.

✓ To be able to discuss the different places that they can access help if needed.

LESSON PLAN

➢ Ask the children to think about their class baby and identify a time when they needed help. What strategies did they use? What happened if their parent didn't respond?

For those classrooms not able to undertake the Circles for Learning Project, video clips or photographs can be used to support the discussion around the topic and stimulate thoughts and ideas from the children and young people.

Task

KS1: To create a Resilience Tree.
KS2/3: To create a Resilience Tree.
   To be able to identify people or places they can get help if needed and skills they have developed which can help them manage life's ups and downs.

KS1

1. Read *The Hugging Tree*.

2. Discuss what enabled the tree to hold onto the rocks and grow.

Copyright material from Alison Waterhouse (2019), *Self-Discovery*, Routledge

Developing resilience

3. Introduce the word resilience – keeping going even when things get tough.

4. Ask the children to share a time when they found something difficult. What strategies did they use?

5. Make a list on the board and discuss the ones most commonly used and the ones that only a few use. How did they learn these?

6. Give each of the children a tree. On the roots write people in their lives that help and support them.

7. On the trunk, write or draw the strategies they use when things get tough.

8. On the branches, draw groups that they are part of. These could be Rainbows, School Team, Church etc.

KS2/3

1. Ask the children to work in pairs and identify the skills that they have which make them strong/courageous/resilient.

2. Ask the children to think of as many places as they can where they could get help and support. Include Childline and Samaritans, teachers, TAs.

3. Fill in the Resilience Tree.

4. Add places that you can get help and support for the roots. Include adults in your life that you can count on.

5. For the trunk add the skills that they have developed to make them strong, courageous and resilient.

6. On the branches draw leaves and put friends and groups that they are part of.

7. Ask the children to share a time when things got difficult but they managed to deal with it. Share the strategies they used to support themselves.

8. Make a list of these on the board and discuss.

9. Ask the children to share one that they have never used but would like to have a go at over the coming term. What do they need to be able to achieve this?

RESOURCES

1. Sticky notes

2. Plain paper and pens

Developing resilience

3. Tree picture

4. *The Hugging Tree* by Jill Neimark and Nicole Wong

IMPORTANT POINTS

We learn new skills when we stretch ourselves or have to manage new things.

There are many places to go for help and support.

Resilience is something that keeps growing.

LEARNING LINKS

Speaking and listening, collaboration, information processing, questioning, observation, creativity, planning and organisation, teamwork.

REFLECTION

Questions:

Positive comment from child:

Positive comment from adult:

LEARNING DIMENSIONS		SOCIAL & EMOTIONAL SKILLS	
Strategic awareness	🟧	Emotional literacy	🟩
Learning relationships		Neuroscience	
Curiosity	🟧	Self-regulation	
Creativity	🟧	Self-development	🟩
Meaning making	🟧		
Changing & learning	🟧		
Resilience	🟩		

Developing resilience

Developing resilience

Resilience snakes and ladders

SESSION OBJECTIVES

To understand that we have the power to influence our future by learning from our past.

SESSION OUTCOMES

✓ To explore our past, present and future and see what we can learn from how we experience them.

✓ To promote feelings of potency and that the young people can make their own future happen.

LESSON PLAN

➤ Ask the children to think about their class baby observations and to remember a time when the baby showed resilience.

➤ Collect definitions of resilience and examples from the children and young people.

For those classrooms not able to undertake the Circles for Learning Project, video clips or photographs can be used to support the discussion around the topic and stimulate thoughts and ideas from the children and young people.

Task

KS2/3: To create a snakes and ladders game. The snakes represent the negative things that have happened in life. The ladders represent the positive things that have happened. The game represents the ups and downs that have been experienced in life. When introducing this be very clear with the children that they should only use things that they feel comfortable with sharing and that there may be up and downs that they have experienced that they do not wish to share.

1. Using the template draw 5 ladders on the board and 5 snakes.

2. Number the snakes and ladders to correspond to life events which they enter on the grid under the appropriate snake or ladder.

Copyright material from Alison Waterhouse (2019), *Self-Discovery*, Routledge

Developing resilience

3. Give the event a score out of 10.

4. The snake events have brought you down. These might be breaking your leg and being in hospital for 4 weeks. This might merit an 8. Or failing your biology test last week, which although a pain wasn't drastic in their minds.

5. Under the ladders write the 5 situations that have made them feel positive. This might be winning their football league or going on holiday with a friend which might merit an 8 or getting the trainers they wanted for their birthday which might be a 3.

6. When they have completed the 5 events for each snake or ladder, add up the scores and see which one comes out on top. How could they improve this in the future?

7. The score can show a life attitude and can be linked to how they see their life.

8. Remind the young people of the reframing exercise they completed.

9. Look at optimism or pessimism and work out which way they think – can they challenge their thinking? Can they now take each negative event and think about something positive that came out of it? e.g. When I was in hospital I had to miss the school camping trip (negative). However, because I was in hospital Mum and Dad felt sorry for me and bought me a new computer game that I had wanted.

RESOURCES

1. Snakes and ladders template
2. Table for snakes and ladders with score column
3. Plain paper and pens
4. Felt pens and markers

IMPORTANT POINTS

Our resilience can be linked to how we perceive things.

Pessimistic and optimistic thinking can be tamed or strengthened.

LEARNING LINKS

Speaking and listening, collaboration, information processing, questioning, observation, creativity, planning and organisation, teamwork.

Developing resilience

REFLECTION

Questions:

Positive comment from child:

Positive comment from adult:

LEARNING DIMENSIONS		SOCIAL & EMOTIONAL SKILLS	
Strategic awareness	🟧	Emotional literacy	🟩
Learning relationships	🟧	Neuroscience	
Curiosity	🟧	Self-regulation	
Creativity	🟧	Self-development	🟩
Meaning making	🟧		
Changing & learning	🟧		
Resilience	🟩		

100	99	98	97	96	95	94	93	92	91
81	82	83	84	85	86	87	88	89	90
80	79	78	77	76	75	74	73	72	71
61	62	63	64	65	66	67	68	69	70
60	59	58	57	56	55	54	53	52	51
41	42	43	44	45	46	47	48	49	50
40	39	38	37	36	35	34	33	32	31
21	22	23	24	25	26	27	28	29	30
20	19	18	17	16	15	14	13	12	11
1	2	3	4	5	6	7	8	9	10

Total   **Total**

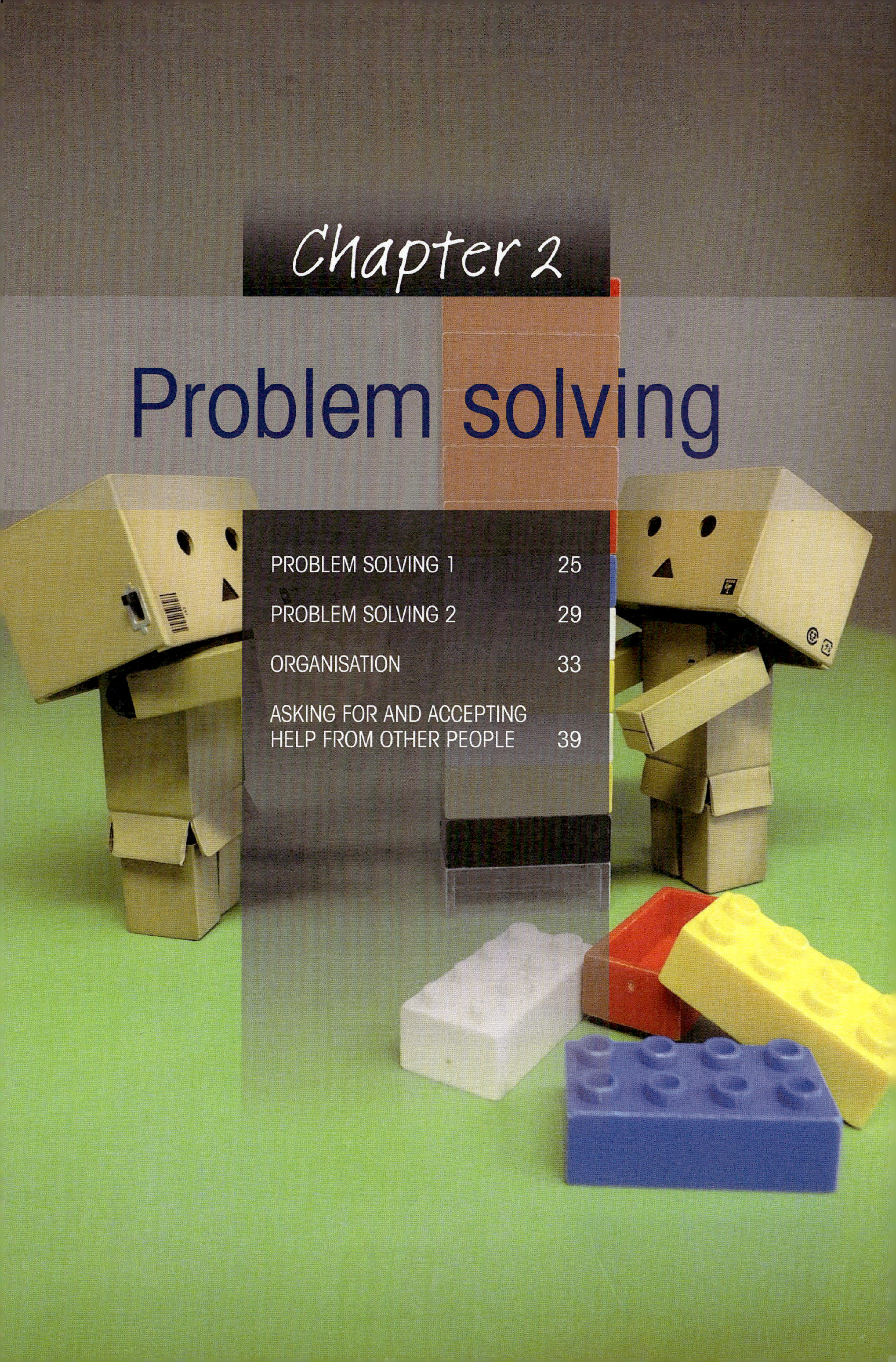

Chapter 2

Problem solving

PROBLEM SOLVING 1	25
PROBLEM SOLVING 2	29
ORGANISATION	33
ASKING FOR AND ACCEPTING HELP FROM OTHER PEOPLE	39

Problem solving 1

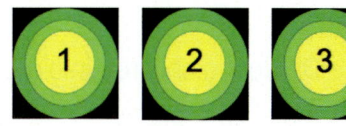

SESSION OBJECTIVES

To identify and explore the skills that make a good problem solver.

SESSION OUTCOMES

- ✓ To identify the emotions we experience when we have a problem to solve.
- ✓ To create a poster to celebrate problem-solving skills KS2/3.

LESSON PLAN

➢ Share a clip or remind the children of a time when their class baby was trying to do something difficult.

➢ What strategies did they use?

   Turn to their parent

   Get cross and hit or throw something

   Turn away

   Try a different way

   Make a sound to attract their parent's attention

Task

KS1: To identify the different emotions we experience when we are trying to solve a problem.
KS2/3: To identify the different strategies we can use when we are solving a problem.
   To identify the different emotions that we may experience when we are solving a problem.
   To become aware of the self-talk that we undertake when we are trying to solve a problem.
   To create a poster to celebrate problem-solving skills.

Problem solving

KS1/2

1. Divide the children into groups of 4. Give each of the children within the group a different matchstick puzzle.

2. Ask them to work on the puzzle.

3. After 1 minute, ask them to share the emotion they are feeling and write this on the board. Ask them to share what they are telling themselves as they work and record this in speech bubbles. Colour positive and negative.

4. After 5 minutes ask the children to go and sit in groups where they each have the same puzzle.

5. Ask them to share what they have been doing.

6. What does it feel like to talk to others about the puzzle?

7. Discuss what they have learnt about problem solving.

KS2/3

1. Divide the children into groups of 4.

2. Give each child within the group a different matchstick puzzle.

3. Ask the children to try and work out the puzzle.

4. Ask them to record their initial feelings and then stop them every minute to explore how they feel and what their self-talk is like. Record positive self-talk and negative self-talk.

5. After 5 minutes, ask the young people to sit with the other people who have their puzzle.

6. Share the different strategies that they used to work out the puzzle:

   Looking and thinking
   Trying things out
   Watching others
   Self-talk – 'Come on, you can do it.'
   Think about something else – take a break
   Ask for a clue

7. Ask the young people to create a poster in pairs that shows the different strategies that can be used to problem-solve.

Problem solving

RESOURCES

1. Sticky notes
2. Matchstick puzzles
3. Matchsticks
4. Plain paper and pens
5. Speech bubbles
6. A3 paper
7. Felt pens and markers

IMPORTANT POINTS

- Problem-solving skills can be developed with practice.
- Positive self-talk is a useful skill to develop.

LEARNING LINKS

Speaking and listening, collaboration, information processing, questioning, observation, creativity, planning and organisation, teamwork.

REFLECTION

Questions:

Positive comment from child:

Positive comment from adult:

Problem solving

LEARNING DIMENSIONS		SOCIAL & EMOTIONAL SKILLS	
Strategic awareness	🟧	Emotional literacy	🟩
Learning relationships		Neuroscience	
Curiosity	🟧	Self-regulation	
Creativity	🟧	Self-development	🟩
Meaning making	🟧		
Changing & learning	🟧		
Resilience	🟩		

Problem solving

Problem solving 2

SESSION OBJECTIVES

To explore different ways of dealing with problems.

To explore other people's thoughts and ideas about different situations.

To understand that being able to problem-solve is a skill that impacts on resilience.

SESSION OUTCOMES

✓ To create a range of solutions to a problem and then choose the best way to deal with the issue.

✓ To explore a problem from different perspectives.

LESSON PLAN

➢ Ask the children to think about their class baby and identify a time when the parent talked about some of the problems that they had to deal with.

Task

KS2/3: To discuss and create a range of possible solutions to the problem scenarios.

KS2/3

1. Put the children into groups of 3 or 4 and ask them to discuss one of the problem scenarios. Ask them to create as many solutions as possible. The solutions can be as creative as they would like. By each solution ask the children to write the consequence if they were to use this solution.

2. Ask the children to choose the solution that they feel would work best. The Golden Rule is that no one can be physically or emotionally hurt.

3. Ask them to qualify why they feel that this is the best solution and the outcomes it will achieve.

Problem solving

RESOURCES

1. Sticky notes
2. Plain paper and pens
3. Problem scenarios
4. Problem page from a teenage magazine
5. Details of Childline, Samaritans and other support organisations

IMPORTANT POINTS

Problem-solving is a powerful skill that supports us in developing resilience.

If we believe we can manage and deal with situations then this mindset will enable us to.

LEARNING LINKS

Speaking and listening, collaboration, information processing, questioning, observation, creativity, planning and organisation, teamwork.

REFLECTION

Questions:

Positive comment from child:

Positive comment from adult:

LEARNING DIMENSIONS		SOCIAL & EMOTIONAL SKILLS	
Strategic awareness		Emotional literacy	
Learning relationships		Neuroscience	
Curiosity		Self-regulation	
Creativity		Self-development	
Meaning making			
Changing & learning			
Resilience			

PROBLEM-SOLVING

PROBLEM 1

I feel really fed up and betrayed by my friend. We are both in Year 7 and came to Windgate Secondary School from the same Primary school. We have known each other since we were in Year 2. Over the last few weeks though Ben has started to hang around with us. Ben lives near my friend Pete and at the weekend they both went out without me and they have been talking about it all day in school. It has made me really mad and fed up because I wasn't invited and I've had to listen to them go on about it all day. I don't know what Ben thinks of me but I get the feeling he wants Pete all to himself and is trying to get me to go away.

PROBLEM 2

Tanya is a friend of mine, she lives just around the corner from me and we often walk to and from school together. I've only known her for a short time, really since she joined the school about a year ago. She's being picked on at lunch time and bullied by some of the older girls in our year. They pick on her because of where her family come from and the fact that she wasn't born in this country. I don't like it but I'm frightened of the girls. If I say something they might start picking on me. When they pick on Tanya I walk away quickly before they start on me. I think it's really unkind but I don't know what to do. I keep thinking that I should say something or stand up for her as I can see it is making her really unhappy. If I do say something they might know it was me and then start to pick on me too.

PROBLEM 3

Jax is my best friend but the trouble is his girlfriend keeps flirting with me when he's not looking or isn't around. I try to ignore her but I'm really worried someone's going to tell him and he will think that I am chasing her. It's got worse this week as she has got my phone number and keeps texting me. I ignore the texts but I'm really worried that Jax will find out she's been texting me and will think I've been talking to her behind his back.

PROBLEM 4

My Mum and Dad split up over a year ago due to my Dad having an affair with a woman he worked with. My Mum was really upset. She was really sad and cried a lot for ages. I had to look after my younger brother as on some days she wouldn't get out of bed. The trouble is Dad has now stopped seeing this woman and has asked me to help him get back with Mum. I don't want her to get hurt again and so I don't know what to do. I don't know if I can trust my Dad again after what he did.

Problem solving

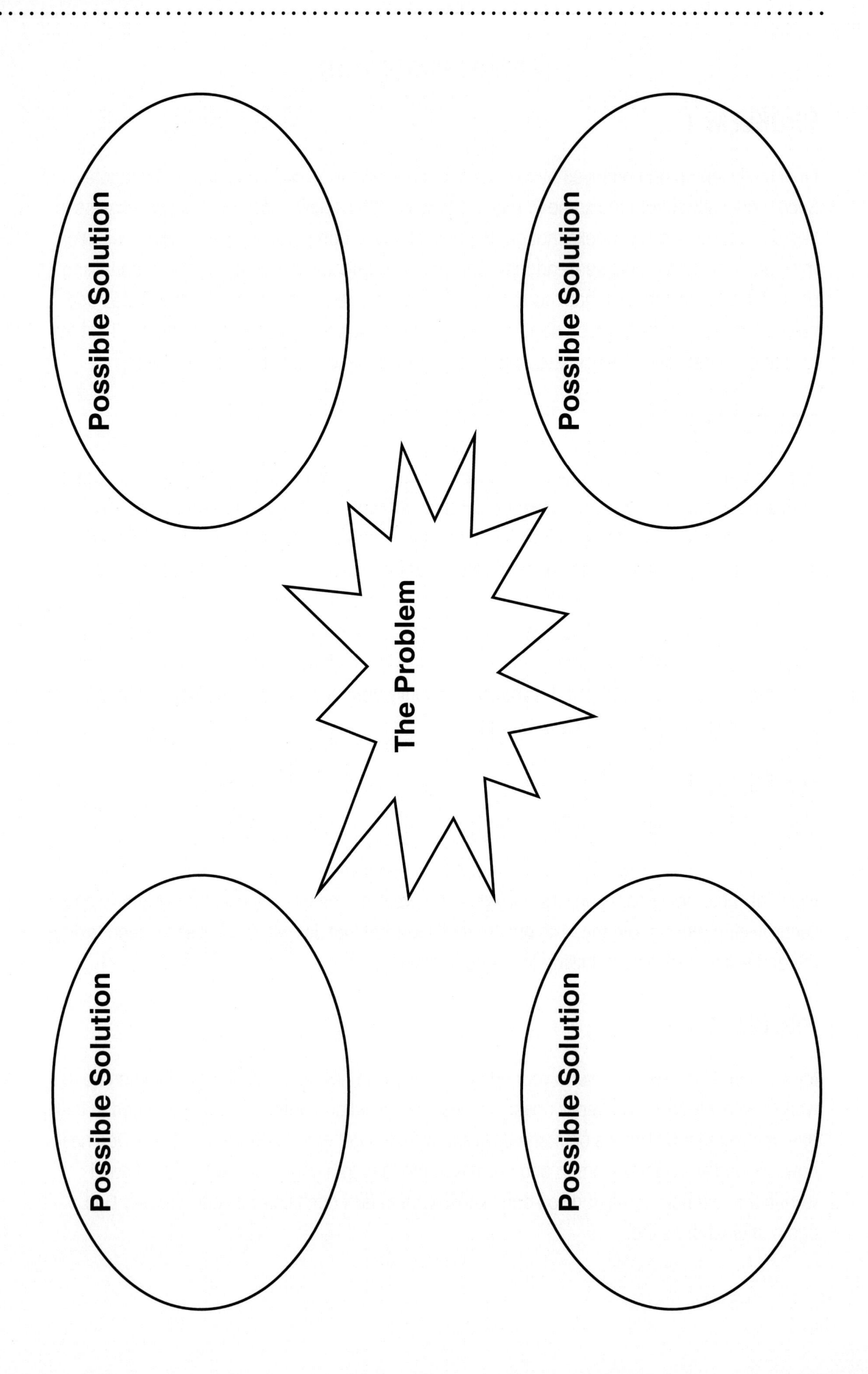

Possible Solution

Possible Solution

The Problem

Possible Solution

Possible Solution

Problem solving

Organisation

SESSION OBJECTIVES

To explore different strategies for getting organised.

SESSION OUTCOMES

✓ To identify strategies that support our way of working and help us become more organised.

LESSON PLAN

➢ Ask the children to think about their class baby and identify a time when they saw how organised their parent had to be.

➢ Ask them to think of the things they have seen the parent carry in their baby bag.

Task

KS1: To create a flow diagram or picture sequence to show how to make a cup of tea.
KS2/3: To create a flow diagram to show how to organise a 'Day in the Life of a Teenager'.

KS1

1. Divide the children into groups and ask them to put a series of pictures in the correct order. Ask the group to tell the story from the pictures.

2. Working with the children, create a flow diagram to show how to make a piece of toast.

3. Ask the children to work in groups on creating a flow diagram to show how to make a cup of tea.

4. Share the diagrams and act out the tea making – follow the diagrams exactly and if there is a mistake, enjoy!

5. Show the children how a piece of work follows a flow diagram pattern. Use this in class to help children understand the process of work.

Copyright material from Alison Waterhouse (2019), *Self-Discovery*, Routledge

Problem solving

KS2/3

1. Divide the children into groups and share the 'My Worst Day' story.

2. Ask the young people to show the story in a flow chart form.

3. Ask them to add to the flow chart strategies that would support the young person in the story to have a better day.

4. Discuss the exercise and explore different ways the young people get themselves organised.

5. Explore how they learnt to do this, and if parents have encouraged or discouraged this. What do they think about this?

6. Explore the phrase 'Stealing the learning'. Why do people do this? What do they hope to achieve? Why do we let them? Stealing the learning is where another person finds watching someone learn too difficult to manage and then does the task for them.

RESOURCES

1. Sticky notes

2. Plain paper and pens

3. Writing a story flow diagram

4. 'My Worst Day' story

5. A range of flow charts showing how to do things

IMPORTANT POINTS

We can learn how to be organised.

We are responsible for our own actions.

LEARNING LINKS

Speaking and listening, collaboration, information processing, questioning, observation, creativity, planning and organisation, teamwork.

Problem solving

REFLECTION

Questions:

Positive comment from child:

Positive comment from adult:

LEARNING DIMENSIONS		SOCIAL & EMOTIONAL SKILLS	
Strategic awareness	🟧	Emotional literacy	🟩
Learning relationships	🟧	Neuroscience	
Curiosity	🟧	Self-regulation	
Creativity	🟧	Self-development	🟩
Meaning making	🟧		
Changing & learning	🟧		
Resilience	🟩		

Problem solving

MY WORST DAY

Today I had the worst day at school ever!! My alarm went off but I was so tired because I'd been up playing on my Xbox until late. I pressed the snooze button – well I thought it was the snooze button but obviously not as it then didn't go off again. My sister and Mum shouting at each other finally woke me up. I leapt out of bed to have a shower but my sister had just finished and there was no hot water – Ahhhh!

I rushed back to my room and quickly got dressed – well I tried to, there were no clean socks in my drawer so I had to crawl about on the floor trying to find a matching pair. I finally made it downstairs for breakfast only to be shouted at by Mum, who was very stressy, because I was late. I got a bowl for some cereal but my little brother took the milk first and poured it into his cup so there was none left. I decided to leave breakfast as I didn't have time to make toast and there were no breakfast biscuits left in the box.

I picked up my bag and ran out the front door – as I went I was thinking about my day – ahhh! PE this afternoon and no PE kit. I raced back indoors and grabbed my bag from the floor in the hall. I looked inside, it was all still wet and muddy from the other day. I asked Mum to write me a note but she said no. It was my responsibility to get myself organised and she was fed up of chasing around after me. I decided to shove it into my bag just in case but decided to think of an excuse about why I couldn't do PE on the way to school. Then I remembered. History homework – bring in the oldest thing in your house. I mean what sort of homework is that!! Frantically I ran around the house trying to think about what the oldest thing was that we owned that A. Mum would let me take to school and B. I could carry. I finally decided to take an old tin that I found on the kitchen shelf. It would have to do. At least I wouldn't get told off for forgetting this time. That was what usually happened.

Finally I ran out of the house and down the road. I was going to be lucky if I managed to catch the bus. As I ran round the corner I saw the bus pull away and drive off. Well what did I expect? It was turning into the day from hell. I really didn't know what I had done to deserve it though.

I waited for the next bus but knew that this would mean I would be late for registration. Mr Brown my form teacher was not going to be happy. I had already been late one day this week. As I waited for the bus a group of Year 9 boys came up and started mucking about pushing and shoving each other. One of them lit up a cigarette. I tried to keep my head down and not get involved. Finally the bus came and I got on. The boys sat near me and carried on mucking about. The driver yelled at them to stop, telling them he would kick them off if they didn't behave. He looked at me and frowned. He must have thought I was one of them. Finally we got to school. I leapt off and ran through the gates. Mrs Taylor was on duty. She thought I was with the group of boys who had been mucking around on the bus and told us all to report to the office as we were all late. When I got there the secretary gave me an earful for being late, and gave me a long lecture on it being my responsibility to get to school on time and that I was letting myself down and wasting my education. I checked my homework planner and ran to

Problem solving

maths. As I crashed through the door I got told to be quiet and that the test had started. What test? Did I know about a test? Eventually a little thought at the back of my mind reminded me that we had been told there would be a test on Wednesday, and yes today was Wednesday, and no I hadn't revised. I searched through my bag for a pen – nothing there; I remembered putting my pencil case on my desk in my room. That was where it still was. I put my hand up and eventually the teacher gave me one, grumbling that I really needed to get myself organised.

Finally the test was over and I escaped to English; the teacher was away and had set some reading of the book we were studying. I sat and relaxed. I was so hungry my stomach kept rumbling. Not long to break but then I realised I hadn't picked up any money. No break snack and no lunch then. The day really was the pits.

Finally I got to break. I managed to scrounge a packet of crisps off my friend but everyone kept winding me up and I wasn't in the mood. They all said I was bad tempered and finally went off and left me on my own.

The next lesson was History. That was alright, I had that covered. I sat at the back and smiled. I had the old tin in my bag. Mr Dixon asked for our homework – I got out the tin. The others got out their History books and Mr Dixon came round and collected them. He tapped my tin: 'Well remembered Toby, you're a week early! Have you got the answers to the questionnaire I set last lesson though?' I tried to explain but he wouldn't listen so I got a lunchtime detention.

The day was really turning out to be a complete nightmare from start to finish. After lunch I had PE. I tried to tell the PE teacher about my kit but he said it was my responsibility and not my Mum's and that until I got myself organised I couldn't play on the football team. Well that was the last straw. I saw red and stormed off. I had had enough. I walked out and ran up to the field where I sat up the tree hiding. I got down at the end of school and hoped to sneak out by the back gate but Mrs Taylor was there and told me that the Head of Year had phoned my Mum and wanted to see us both, tomorrow morning at 9 o'clock. Mum was going to be furious.

Problem solving

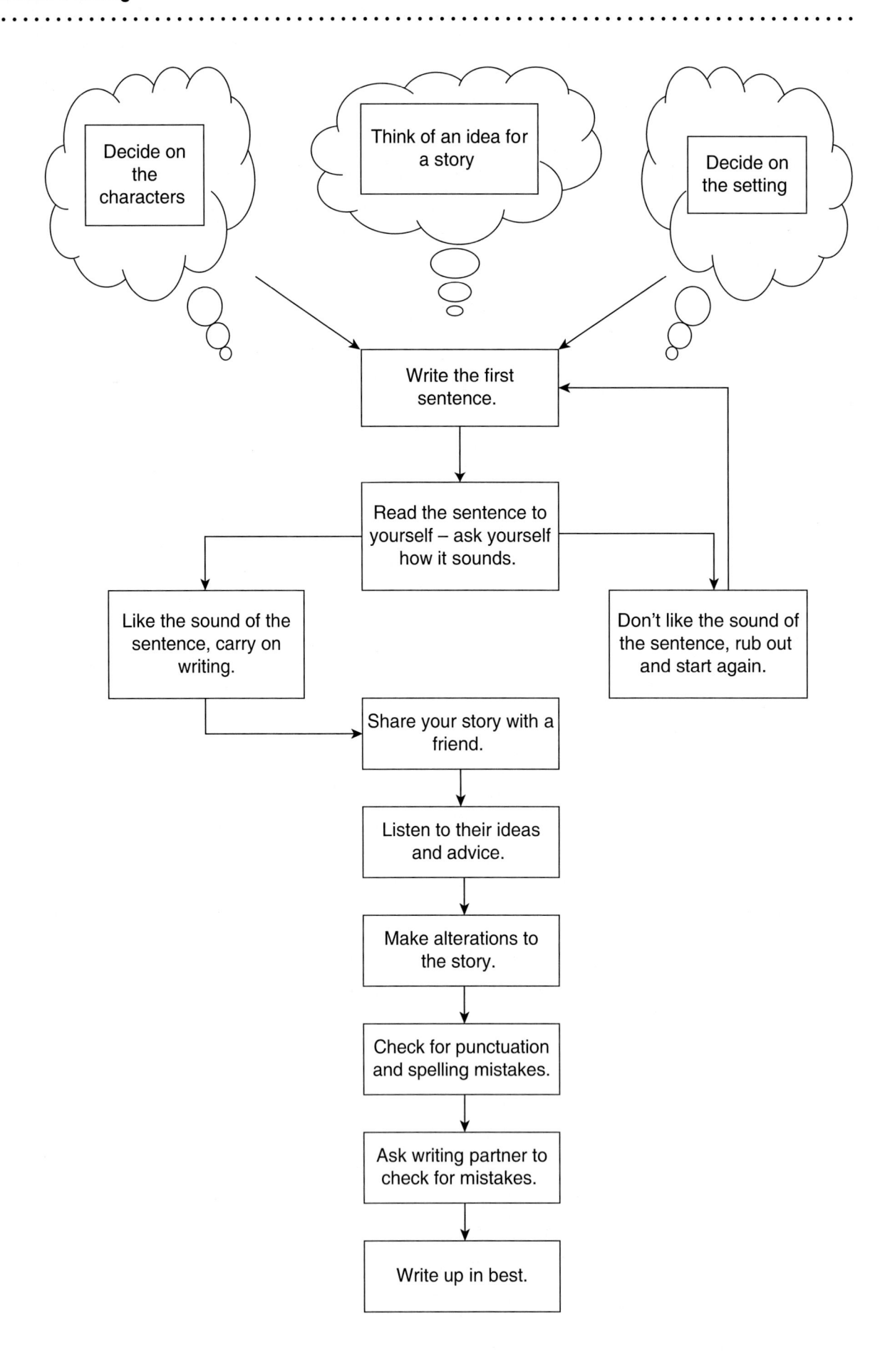

- Decide on the characters
- Think of an idea for a story
- Decide on the setting

↓

Write the first sentence.

↓

Read the sentence to yourself – ask yourself how it sounds.

- Like the sound of the sentence, carry on writing.
- Don't like the sound of the sentence, rub out and start again. *(returns to Write the first sentence.)*

↓

Share your story with a friend.

↓

Listen to their ideas and advice.

↓

Make alterations to the story.

↓

Check for punctuation and spelling mistakes.

↓

Ask writing partner to check for mistakes.

↓

Write up in best.

Problem solving

Asking for and accepting help from other people

SESSION OBJECTIVES

To enable children to explore and identify who they can turn to for support when they need it.

SESSION OUTCOMES

✓ To identify people we can turn to for support when we need to.

LESSON PLAN

➢ Ask the children to think about their class baby and identify a time when they sought help or support. Ask the children the ways the baby asked for support – actions and words.

➢ Discuss how the parent responded to the request for support. Explore what it must be like to have experienced an adult think about you and respond to your needs. How would that make you think about people and the world that you lived in.

Task

KS1: To identify times when they have needed help and received it.
　　　To identify ways that they have obtained the help that they have needed.
　　　To identify the people they have around them to support them.
　　　To create a 'Hand of Helpers'.
KS2/3: To identify times when they have needed help and received it.
　　　　To identify ways that they have obtained the help that they have needed.

Problem solving

To identify the people they have around them to support them.
To create a personal specification for a Peer Support Person.

KS1

1. Ask the children to divide a piece of A4 paper in 4.

2. On one quarter ask them to draw a picture of a time when one of their friends helped them.

3. On the other quarter ask them to draw a picture of a time when they helped a child at school.

4. On the third quarter ask them to draw a picture of a time when an adult helped them at school.

5. On the last quarter ask them to draw a time when an adult helped them at home.

6. Ask the children to draw a 'Hand of Helpers'. Ask the children to draw around their hand. Put a small face at the end of each finger and then write a person who helps them along each finger. In the palm they can write 'A good helper is . . .'

KS2

1. Ask the children to think about the different times that they have needed support.

2. Ask the children to work in pairs and go through the questions and think of people they could talk to: older sister, best friend, etc.

3. Once they have answered the questions, ask them what sort of person makes a good person to ask for help from. What qualities do they need? A good listener, not judgmental, loyal, trustworthy, kind, a good problem-solver etc.

4. Discuss organisations that support different groups of people. Share information about Childline and the Samaritans.

5. In pairs ask the children to write a personal specification for an ideal support person.

6. Discuss how difficult it can be to ask for help – explore ways of doing this – verbally, by email or text, our behaviour etc.

7. Discuss what it is like to accept help.

Questions KS1

1. A person you can talk to about a problem at school?

2. A person who can help you with a problem in the playground?

3. A person who can help you learn your spellings or practise your reading?

Problem solving

4. A person who helps you if you get upset?

5. A person who can help you if you have an argument with your friend?

6. A person who can help you if you feel frightened?

Questions KS2

1. A person who you can tell a secret to?

2. A person who you can talk to about a problem?

3. A person who can help you if you fall out with your friends?

4. A person who can help you if you are picked on at school?

5. A person who can help you if you argue with your Mum and Dad?

6. A person who can help you if you feel upset and sad?

Questions KS3

1. A person you can talk to about an argument with your boyfriend/girlfriend?

2. A person you can talk to about a problem at home?

3. A person who can help you if you get picked on on your way to school?

4. A person you can talk to if you feel overwhelmed by things?

5. A person you can talk to if you are worried and anxious?

6. A person you can call if you find yourself in a difficult situation?

RESOURCES

1. Sticky notes

2. Personal specification

3. Plain paper and pens

IMPORTANT POINTS

We have people around us who can help if we ask them.

Sometimes it takes courage to ask for help and to accept it.

Problem solving

LEARNING LINKS

Emotional literacy, working with others, self-development, collaboration.

REFLECTION

Questions:

Positive comment from child:

Positive comment from adult:

LEARNING DIMENSIONS		SOCIAL & EMOTIONAL SKILLS	
Strategic awareness	🟧	Emotional literacy	🟩
Learning relationships		Neuroscience	
Curiosity	🟧	Self-regulation	
Creativity	🟧	Self-development	🟩
Meaning making	🟧		
Changing & learning	🟧		
Resilience	🟩		

Chapter 3
Emotional reactivity

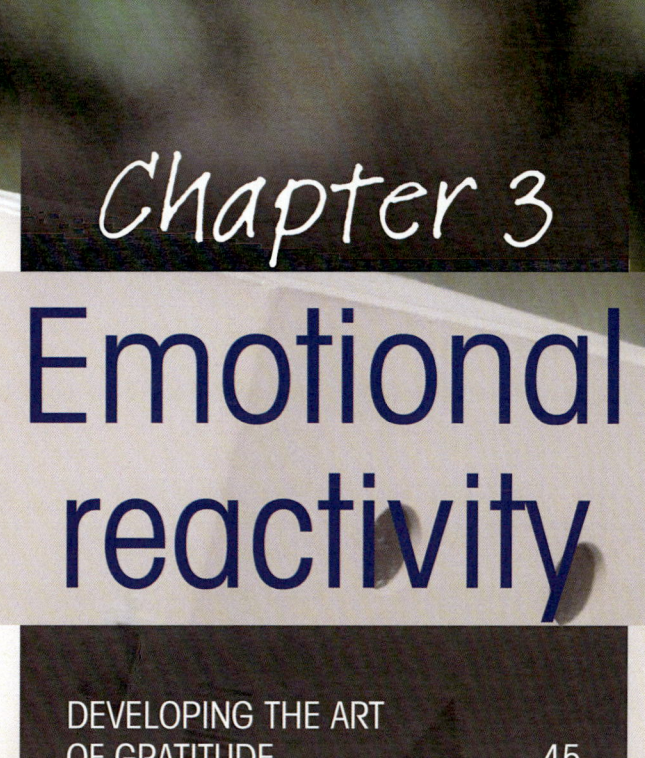

DEVELOPING THE ART OF GRATITUDE	45
THOUGHTS, FEELINGS, ACTIONS TRIANGLE: SELF-LIMITING BELIEFS	51
THOUGHTS, FEELINGS, ACTIONS TRIANGLE: THINKING ERRORS	57
MY COMFORT ZONE	61

Emotional reactivity

Developing the art of gratitude

SESSION OBJECTIVES

To encourage children and young people to find the positive things that have happened in the day.

To enable children and young people to develop the ability of being grateful.

SESSION OUTCOMES

- ✓ To identify the different things that have gone well that day.

- ✓ To identify things that have happened that have been good.

LESSON PLAN

➢ Ask the children to think about their class baby and what they enjoy. How do they know that they enjoy this?

➢ What gives the baby most pleasure? How do they know? What difference do they think these things will make to the baby as they develop?

For those classrooms not able to undertake the Circles for Learning Project, video clips or photographs can be used to support the discussion around the topic and stimulate thoughts and ideas from the children and young people.

Task
KS1: To create a suitcase/bag of things that they are grateful about.
KS2/3: To create a pin board of things they are grateful for.

KS1/2
1. Discuss the word 'grateful' and what it means.

2. Ask the children to share things that they are pleased with or grateful for – this might be their teddy bear, the way their dog greets them or the way their Mum tickles their toes in the morning to wake them up.

Emotional reactivity

3. Ask the children to work in pairs to share three things that they are grateful for today.

4. Discuss as a class.

5. Ask the children to draw all the things that they are grateful for today around their suitcase.

6. Create a grateful gallery.

7. Use the picture frame each day to put something in that the class is grateful for.

KS3

1. Discuss what the word 'grateful' means.

2. Think of things that we have enjoyed that morning, things that have made them smile – write a list together. Ask the young people to think about one of the things that they have enjoyed. A cup of coffee, a hot chocolate – something that made them smile. If they have had a horrid morning, ask them to think of something over the past few days that has made them smile.

3. Ask them how they feel just thinking about it. They will get a feeling similar to the one they experienced before. Ask the young people to think of a lemon – they should all feel this in their mouth. Their body reacts.

4. What do they think that reminding themselves of things that made them smile does to the body?

5. Discuss the production of hormones that are released by the body when we are happy – serotonin and dopamine.

6. Create a 'gratitude' or 'things that make me smile' board.

7. Put one of the things that make you smile onto a pebble and carry this around in your pocket as a gratitude token.

RESOURCES

1. Sticky notes

2. Plain paper and pens

3. Photo frame

4. Gratitude pin board

5. Pebbles

6. Glue

7. Suitcase

IMPORTANT POINTS

If we can focus on the things that make us happy then we can alter our state of mind and become positive.

LEARNING LINKS

Self-development, empathy, working with others, emotional literacy, team work.

REFLECTION

Questions:

Positive comment from child:

Positive comment from adult:

LEARNING DIMENSIONS		SOCIAL & EMOTIONAL SKILLS	
Strategic awareness	🟧	Emotional literacy	🟩
Learning relationships		Neuroscience	
Curiosity	🟧	Self-regulation	
Creativity		Self-development	🟩
Meaning making	🟧		
Changing & learning	🟧		
Resilience	🟩		

Emotional reactivity

Emotional reactivity

Emotional reactivity

Emotional reactivity

Thoughts, Feelings, Actions Triangle: Self-limiting beliefs

SESSION OBJECTIVES

To understand how your early beliefs impact on your thoughts, feelings and actions.

SESSION OUTCOMES

- ✓ Thoughts, feelings, actions magic circle and negative trap.

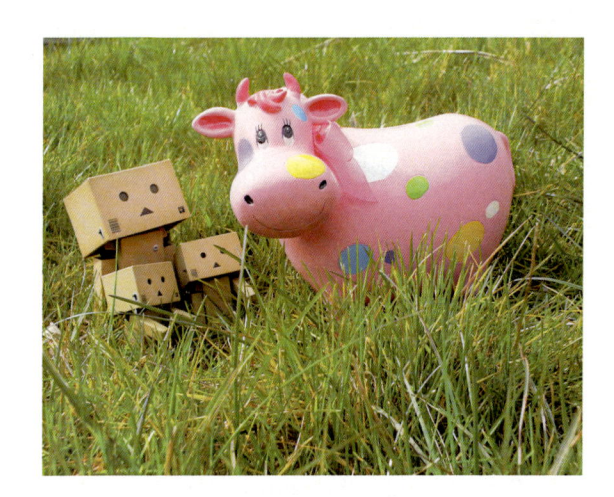

LESSON PLAN

- ➢ Ask the children to remember a time they had observed the parent giving their class baby a label.

- ➢ Discuss the work done on labels and how they can cause us to have a positive core belief or a negative one.

For those classrooms not able to undertake the Circles for Learning Project, video clips or photographs can be used to support the discussion around the topic and stimulate thoughts and ideas from the children and young people.

Task

KS1: To make a class poster that shows a range of strategies to help us keep going when the going gets tough.
KS2: To create in groups a poster that identifies strategies that help us manage our negative beliefs or negative self-talk.

KS1

1. Read the story *Ish* by Peter Reynolds.

Emotional reactivity

2. Discuss how the little boy felt after his big brother's comment.

3. How did this affect his behaviour?

4. What happened to change his belief?

5. How can we challenge our beliefs about ourselves?

6. Create a class poster to remind the children of how we can challenge ourselves to believe in ourselves.

7. What would we say to our best friend? Can the children come up with a phrase and then say it to themselves when things get difficult?

KS2

1. Recap on the idea that we are all given labels and that it is our choice whether we keep them or throw them away.

2. Look at the Thoughts, Feelings, Actions Flow Chart and discuss. Ask the young people if they can identify a core belief they have and share it with the group.

3. Ask the young to identify and share some of their automatic thoughts – good and bad.

4. Support the young people to explore what negative thoughts they get and how they make them feel. Pose the question, Are negative thoughts useful?

5. Discuss when they are and when they are not. Record on the board.

6. Focus on when negative thoughts are not useful and ask what people do about them.

7. List the strategies they may include: not listen, ignore, argue, switch off.

8. Other things that you could suggest include turning the volume down, changing the voice – Donald Duck!! Thank your inner self for looking out for you and explain that these thoughts are not helpful at the moment.

9. Ask the young people to make a poster showing the different ways we can challenge our negative self-talk.

RESOURCES

1. Flip chart and pens

2. Sticky notes

3. Paper and pens

4. Coloured pens

Emotional reactivity

5. Thoughts, Feelings, Actions Triangle

6. The Magic Circle and Negative Trap activity sheet

7. Thoughts, Feelings, Actions Flow Chart

8. *Ish* by Peter Reynolds

IMPORTANT POINTS

- Our beliefs impact on what we do, what we believe we can do and therefore on the way we experience the world.

- We can challenge our negative self-talk.

LEARNING LINKS

Speaking and listening, collaboration, information processing, questioning, observation, creativity, planning and organisation, teamwork.

REFLECTION

Questions:

Positive comment from child:

Positive comment from adult:

LEARNING DIMENSIONS		SOCIAL & EMOTIONAL SKILLS	
Strategic awareness	■	Emotional literacy	■
Learning relationships		Neuroscience	
Curiosity		Self-regulation	
Creativity	■	Self-development	■
Meaning making	■		
Changing & learning	■		
Resilience	■		

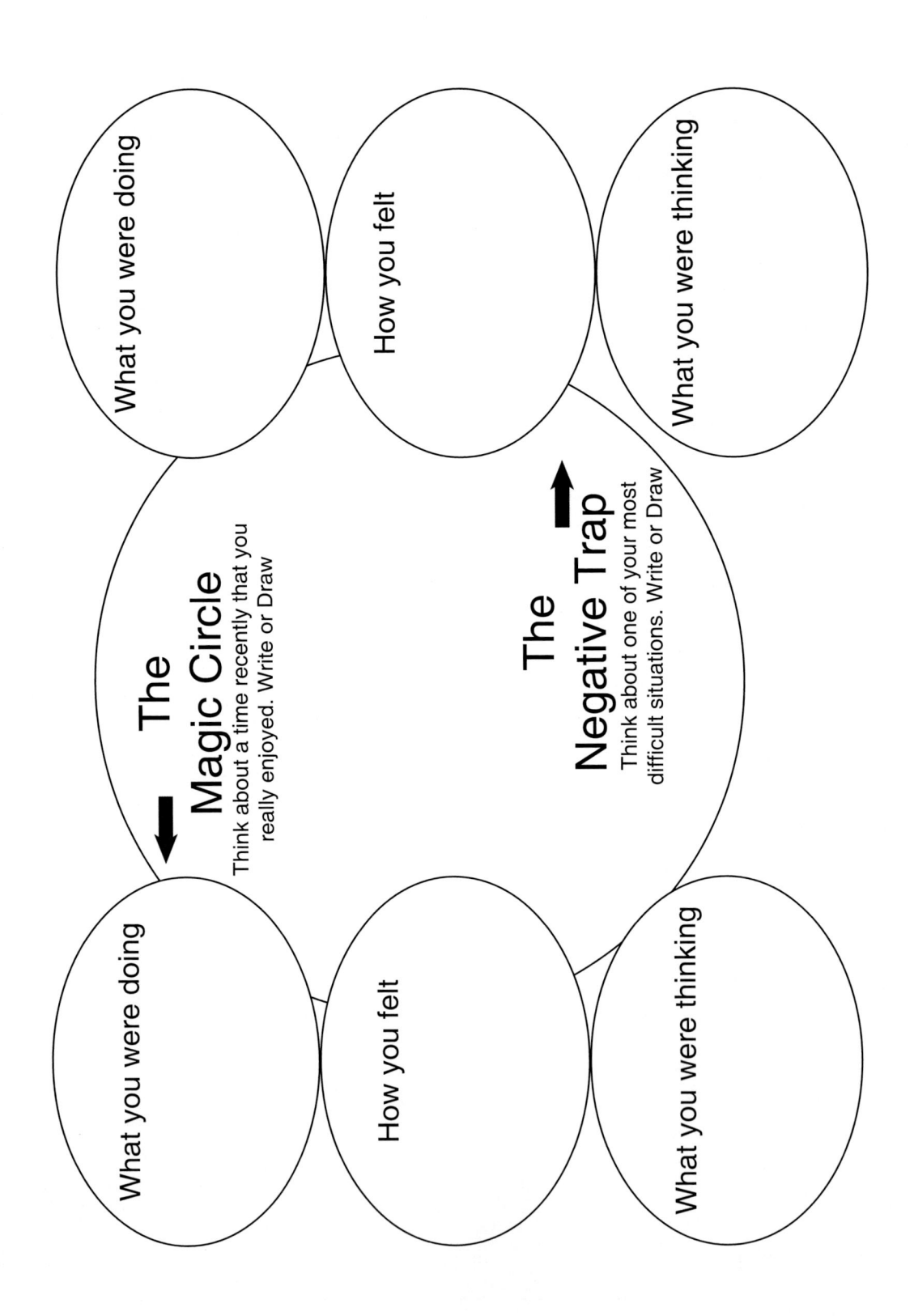

Emotional reactivity

The Magic Circle
Think about a time recently that you really enjoyed. Write or Draw

- What you were doing
- How you felt
- What you were thinking

The Negative Trap
Think about one of your most difficult situations. Write or Draw

- What you were doing
- How you felt
- What you were thinking

Emotional reactivity

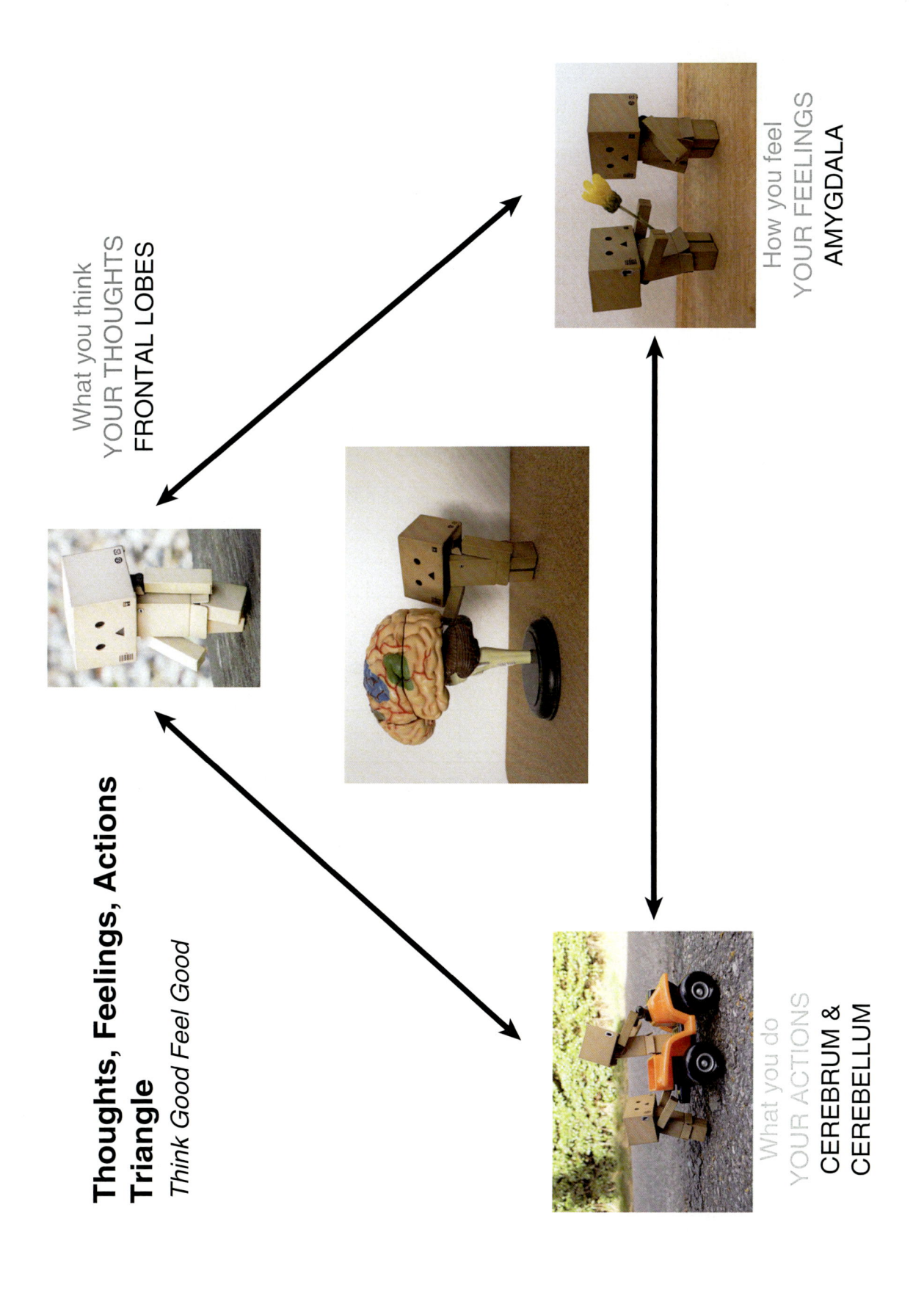

Thoughts, Feelings, Actions Triangle
Think Good Feel Good

What you think
YOUR THOUGHTS
FRONTAL LOBES

How you feel
YOUR FEELINGS
AMYGDALA

What you do
YOUR ACTIONS
CEREBRUM &
CEREBELLUM

Emotional reactivity

Thoughts, Feelings, Actions Flow Chart

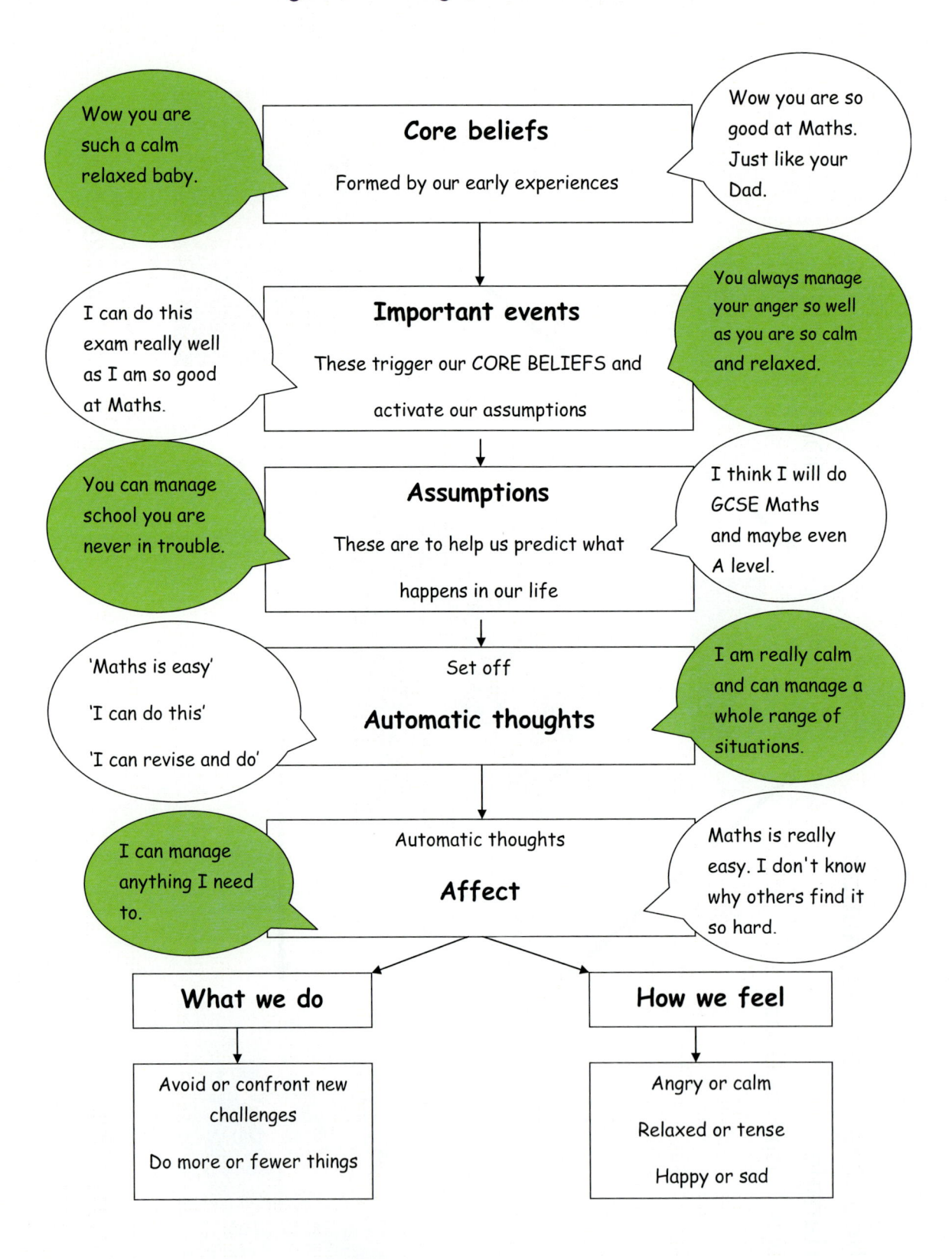

Core beliefs

Formed by our early experiences

- Wow you are such a calm relaxed baby.
- Wow you are so good at Maths. Just like your Dad.

Important events

These trigger our CORE BELIEFS and activate our assumptions

- I can do this exam really well as I am so good at Maths.
- You always manage your anger so well as you are so calm and relaxed.

Assumptions

These are to help us predict what happens in our life

- You can manage school you are never in trouble.
- I think I will do GCSE Maths and maybe even A level.

Set off

Automatic thoughts

- 'Maths is easy'
- 'I can do this'
- 'I can revise and do'
- I am really calm and can manage a whole range of situations.

Automatic thoughts

Affect

- I can manage anything I need to.
- Maths is really easy. I don't know why others find it so hard.

What we do

Avoid or confront new challenges

Do more or fewer things

How we feel

Angry or calm

Relaxed or tense

Happy or sad

Emotional reactivity

Thoughts, Feelings, Actions Triangle: Thinking errors

SESSION OBJECTIVES

To understand how thinking errors can cause us to feel unpleasant and stop us from achieving what we want.

SESSION OUTCOMES

✓ A poster/advert for a magazine to demonstrate thinking errors that can impact on how we live our lives.

LESSON PLAN

➢ Ask the children to remember a time when they heard their class parent give their class baby a label. It might be a positive one – 'Oh you are so very good at building things.' Or it might be a negative one – 'You find building so much more difficult than your sister did. She was building towers when she was 9 months. You are already 12 months and still not doing it.' Ask the children how they think this might influence the baby as the baby grows up.

For those classrooms not able to undertake the Circles for Learning Project, video clips or photographs can be used to support the discussion around the topic and stimulate thoughts and ideas from the children and young people.

Task

KS2/KS3: To create a poster or an advert for a magazine that shows the thinking errors that we can have and how they impact on how we see the world and how we behave.

Remind the children/young people about automatic thoughts and how they can be triggered by our beliefs. Through a range of questions, ask the children to describe the type of negative thoughts that they have experienced when things have gone wrong or are tough.

Emotional reactivity

Share the six different categories with the children and ask them to make a poster/advert for a teen magazine to share these with other young people.

1. Ask the children how we take in information. Explore the senses: Eyes – see, Ears – hear, Mouth – taste, Skin – touch, Nose – smell. Add vestibular and proprioception:

   Vestibular – The vestibular system includes the parts of the inner ear and brain that help control balance and eye movements.
   Proprioception – The sense through which we perceive the position and movement of our body, including our sense of equilibrium and balance, senses that depend on the notion of force.

2. Explore with the children how we can 'hear' information in different ways depending upon how we feel. Can they share examples? Maybe the way Mum or Dad asks them to tidy up their room – sometimes feels like being nagged and other times feels like they just want things to be nice for them.

3. Share the thinking errors sheet with the children and discuss.

4. Can they give examples of when they have thought in these ways? As an adult, share suitable examples with them of thoughts that you may have had.

5. Ask the children to come up with things that people might say that tell them that they are caught up in error thinking.

   Mental filtering: Nothing ever works for me/Nobody ever invites me anywhere.
   Jumping to conclusions: Ella hates me, I know she does/I know Ben and Stan are really angry with me.

6. Divide the class into groups of 4 and ask them to create a poster or advert for a magazine sharing these different thinking errors – they can illustrate with examples and pictures.

7. Share the work and discuss what this has made the children think about.

8. What have they learnt and what will they take away with them?

RESOURCES

1. Large flip chart
2. Pens for flip chart
3. Sticky notes
4. Paper and pens

Emotional reactivity

5. Coloured pens
6. Thoughts, Feelings, Actions Flow Chart
7. The Magic Circle and Negative Trap activity sheet
8. Thinking errors definitions

IMPORTANT POINTS

- Our thoughts can be positive or can be negative and come from our early experiences which have created our beliefs.
- Our thinking errors can influence how we experience the world.

LEARNING LINKS

Speaking and listening, collaboration, information processing, questioning, observation, creativity, planning and organisation, teamwork, creativity.

REFLECTION

Questions:

Positive comment from child:

Positive comment from adult:

LEARNING DIMENSIONS		SOCIAL & EMOTIONAL SKILLS	
Strategic awareness	■	Emotional literacy	■
Learning relationships		Neuroscience	
Curiosity		Self-regulation	
Creativity	■	Self-development	■
Meaning making	■		
Changing & learning	■		
Resilience	■		

Emotional reactivity

THINKING ERRORS OR DISTORTIONS

Thinking errors or distortions make us interpret events in a negative way. Positive events are not noticed or missed and are not accepted or given a positive understanding. This tends to mean that the negative events are the ones noticed and thought about.

Mental filtering is a thinking distortion where we filter things out of our conscious awareness. This is where we choose to focus on the negative things rather than on the positive things in a situation. For example – we choose to focus on what's not going well, mistakes we have made rather than the things that did go well or the achievements we made.

Jumping to conclusions is a thinking distortion where we make irrational assumptions about things. For example, we assume that something will happen in the future. This is called predicting or we assume that we know what someone else is thinking. These assumptions are not based on evidence or facts but are based on our personal feelings and opinions.

Personalisation is a thinking distortion that means we take the blame for everything that goes wrong with or in our life. If things don't work out well or as we hope we immediately blame ourselves. This is not based on any facts or evidence and is not related at all to whether we caused the situation.

Black and white thinking is a thinking distortion where we see things as either good or bad, right or wrong. This tends to mean we only see the extremes of the situation and are not able to recognise that there may be something in the middle or that a situation may have many shades of grey.

Catastrophising is a thinking distortion where we make everything much worse than it is. The problem or situation may be very small; however, if we get into the habit of catastrophizing, we always make problems larger than life. This in turn then makes them truly difficult situations, events or circumstances to overcome.

Overgeneralisation is a thinking distortion where we make broad generalisations. These are often based on a single event from our past experiences which we then use as a basis for making assumptions. For example, whenever you say that 'Everyone always . . . My Mum never . . .', this becomes an overgeneralisation.

Labelling is a thinking distortion where we make global statements about ourselves or others based on behaviour we have experienced. These labels are based on past experiences or personal opinions and not on facts and evidence. For example 'You are a dreadful listener, you never remember anything,' 'You are really bad at maths, your test results are dreadful.'

Emotional reactivity

My comfort zone

SESSION OBJECTIVES

To enable children to identify their different learning zones: My Comfort Zone, My Learning Zone, My Breakthrough Zone, My Meltdown Zone.

To enable children to identify the strategies that they used to achieve something difficult and move into a new zone.

SESSION OUTCOMES

✓ To be able to identify our learning zones.

✓ To be able to identify what strategies we use to move into a different zone.

LESSON PLAN

➢ Ask the children to think about their class baby and identify a time when they persevered and achieved something difficult.

➢ Identify the different zones that the baby went through: Comfort Zone, Learning Zone, Breakthrough Zone.

➢ What stopped them entering the Meltdown Zone?

For those classrooms not able to undertake the Circles for Learning Project, video clips or photographs can be used to support the discussion around the topic and stimulate thoughts and ideas from the children and young people.

Task

KS1: To explore their learning zone and to identify what they need to stretch themselves into the next zone.
KS2/3: To create their own learning zone diagram and show what strategies they use to move into the next one.

Emotional reactivity

KS1

1. Ask the children to work on a puzzle.

2. Stop at stages to check where they are and what they think they need.

3. Ask the children to map where they are.

4. The children can use a small figure and place it in the zone that they are in. On speech bubbles they can write how they are feeling or show a feeling face. Number the positions on the sheet.

5. Hand out a difficult looking puzzle. Map where they are and how they feel.

6. Ask the children what they need to be able to manage.

7. Explore how different people need different things.

8. Create a learning zone picture and ask the children to draw or write what they need when they are being stretched in their learning.

KS2/3

1. Ask the young people to work on a puzzle.

2. Stop at stages to check where they are and what they think they need.

3. Ask them to map where they are on the zone.

4. Hand out a difficult looking puzzle. Map where they are and how they feel.

5. Give verbal instructions. Map where they are and how they feel.

6. Put the instructions on the board so that they can read them when they need to. Map how they feel and what they are thinking.

7. Ask them to read through the puzzle and think about how they might solve it. Map how they feel and which zone they are in.

8. Tell them that you will not be able to help them. Map how they feel and where they are on the zones.

9. Tell them that they have 5 minutes. Map where they are and how they feel.

10. Tell them that there are 5 clues to unlocking the puzzle and that they are on the table on cards. Explain that they can come and read a clue whenever they want to. Map where they are and how they feel.

11. Give them 15 minutes to do the puzzle.

Emotional reactivity

12. Get the children to show what they needed to move from one zone to another – could be environmental – quiet, sitting near a friend – or internal – self-talk reminder, time, access to support, clues etc.

13. Share what they were feeling and what support they found useful and what they have learnt about themselves.

RESOURCES

1. Sticky notes
2. Plain paper and pens
3. Zone sheet
4. Ladders sheet
5. Small figures
6. Puzzle
7. Puzzle clues

IMPORTANT POINTS

We move through zones when learning.

Sometimes we need support to leave our Comfort Zone.

LEARNING LINKS

Speaking and listening, collaboration, information processing, questioning, observation, creativity, planning and organisation, teamwork.

REFLECTION

Questions:

Positive comment from child:

Positive comment from adult:

Emotional reactivity

LEARNING DIMENSIONS		SOCIAL & EMOTIONAL SKILLS	
Strategic awareness	🟧	Emotional literacy	🟩
Learning relationships		Neuroscience	
Curiosity	🟧	Self-regulation	
Creativity	🟧	Self-development	🟩
Meaning making	🟧		
Changing & learning	🟧		
Resilience	🟩		

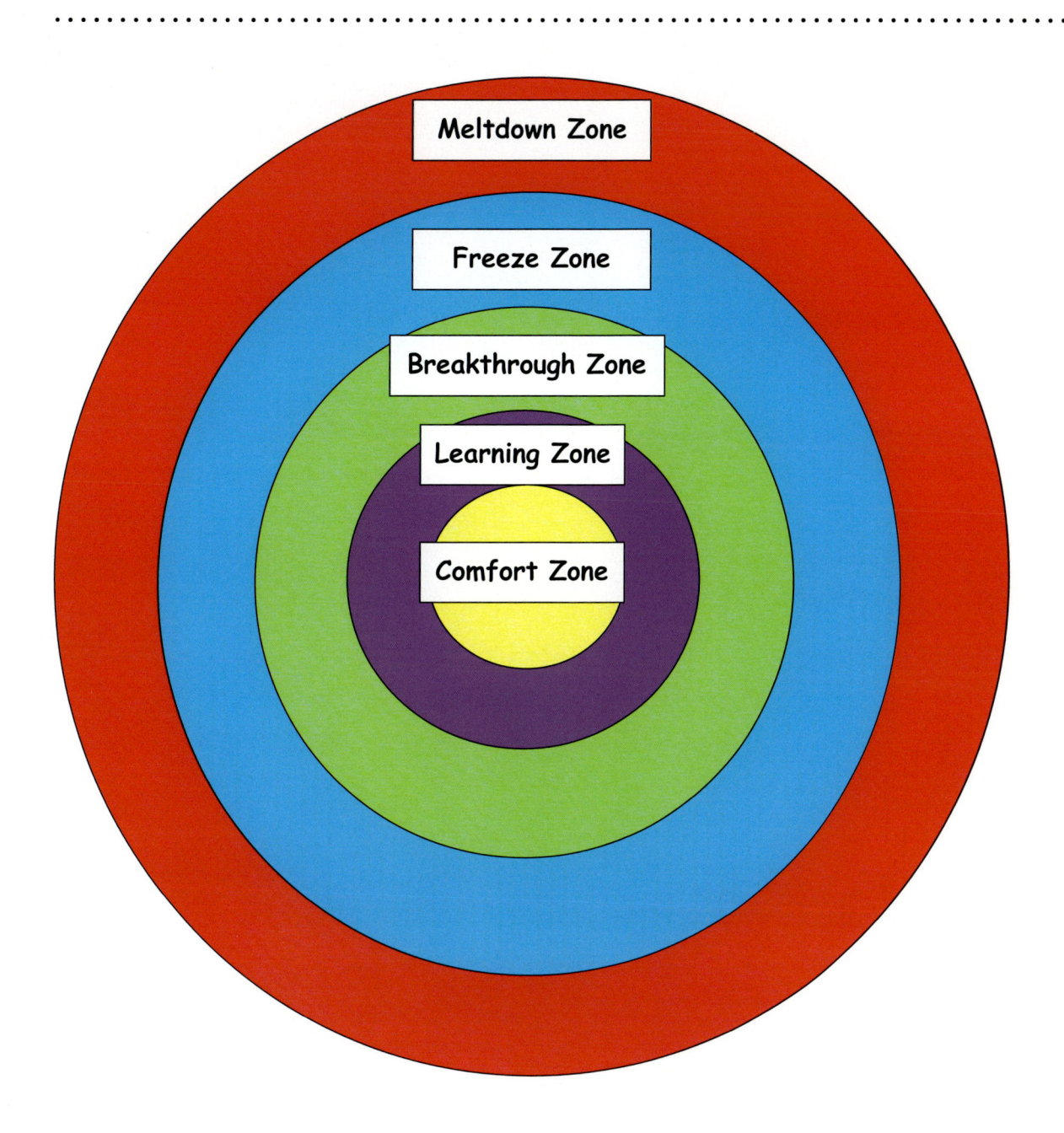

Emotional reactivity

- Meltdown Zone
- Freeze Zone
- Breakthrough Zone
- Learning Zone
- Comfort Zone

Chapter 4

Positive thinking

DEVELOPING POSITIVE SELF-TALK	69
THINK OF IT IN ANOTHER WAY: REFRAMING	72
THE BEST MISTAKE I EVER MADE!	80
ROSE-TINTED GLASSES	83
THERE IS ONLY ONE PERSON RESPONSIBLE FOR YOUR HAPPINESS	87

Positive thinking

Developing positive self-talk

SESSION OBJECTIVES

To identify the self-talk that we use.

To turn the negative self- talk into positive self-talk.

SESSION OUTCOMES

✓ To be able to create positive self-talk when we need to undertake a difficult task or cope with something hard.

LESSON PLAN

➢ Ask the children to think about what they have learnt about being a parent from the class baby parent?

➢ Was it as easy as people had thought it would be?

➢ How do the parents cope with self-doubt?

For those classrooms not able to undertake the Circles for Learning Project, video clips or photographs can be used to support the discussion around the topic and stimulate thoughts and ideas from the children and young people.

Task

KS1: To identify what messages we give ourselves when we are undertaking a difficult task.
KS2/3: To identify the self-talk we use when we are doing something difficult.
    To change the negative self-talk into something positive.

KS1/2

1. Give the children a puzzle – matchsticks puzzles are good.

2. Ask them to work on the puzzle on their own. Stop the children every once in a while and ask what the talk inside their head is – is it negative or positive? Ask them for examples.

Copyright material from Alison Waterhouse (2019), *Self-Discovery*, Routledge

69

Positive thinking

When they use negative self-talk, how does it make them feel? If they used positive self-talk, how does that make them feel?

3. Read the children the story *The Most Magnificent Thing* by Ashley Spires.

4. Ask the children to give you examples of what the little girl is saying to herself as you read through the story. Focus on the negative self-talk and how that is making her feel.

5. If she was their friend what would they be saying to her?

6. Help them think about changing the negative phrases to positive ones.

7. Ask them to draw a picture of themselves doing the puzzle and put red negative self-talk on one side and green positive self-talk on the other.

8. Ask them how they change the red to the green.

KS3

1. Give the children a puzzle – matchstick puzzles are good.

2. Ask them to work at this on their own for a few minutes.

3. Share the video clip of a 600 m race,

   https://www.youtube.com/watch?v=xjejTQdK5Ol

   Think about the self-talk that is taking place from the athletes.

4. Ask the young people to listen to their own self-talk as they complete the puzzle.

5. Ask the children to share some of the self-talk and then change the message:

   I can't – cut off the 't' and you get 'can' or change it to 'I can't do this YET'.
   I'm no good at this – I can learn how to improve.
   I'm useless at this – I can improve if I practise.
   Set the challenge – one side to come up with the negative – red – and the other to change it – green.

RESOURCES

1. Sticky notes

2. *The Most Magnificent Thing* by Ashley Spires

3. Plain paper and pens

4. Red and green felt tip pens

Positive thinking

5. Paper

6. Video clip of a 600 m race

https://www.youtube.com/watch?v=xjejTQdK5OI (accessed 6 November 2018)

IMPORTANT POINTS

We can change our self-talk from negative to positive.

If we treat ourselves as we would do our friends then we would be much kinder and our self-talk would be more positive.

LEARNING LINKS

Speaking and listening, collaboration, information processing, questioning, observation, creativity, planning and organisation, teamwork.

REFLECTION

Questions:

Positive comment from child:

Positive comment from adult:

LEARNING DIMENSIONS		SOCIAL & EMOTIONAL SKILLS	
Strategic awareness	🟧	Emotional literacy	🟩
Learning relationships		Neuroscience	
Curiosity	🟧	Self-regulation	
Creativity	🟧	Self-development	🟩
Meaning making	🟧		
Changing & learning	🟧		
Resilience	🟩		

Positive thinking

Think of it in another way: Reframing

SESSION OBJECTIVES

To explore how thinking about things in a different way can change how we feel.

SESSION OUTCOMES

- ✓ To understand that by changing the way we think we can change the way we feel.

- ✓ To be able to develop the skill of finding the positive way of thinking about things.

LESSON PLAN

➢ Support the children/young people to remember a time when their class baby was being described by their parent. How did the parent do this?

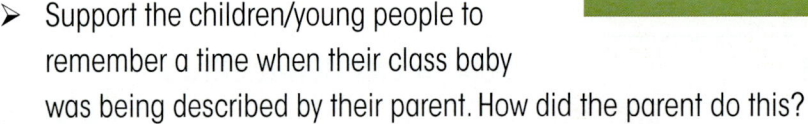

For those classrooms not able to undertake the Circles for Learning Project, video clips or photographs can be used to support the discussion around the topic and stimulate thoughts and ideas from the children and young people.

Task

KS1: To identify the different ways we can think about an event or an experience and link this to how we feel.

KS2/3: To identify the different ways we can think about an event or an experience.
To identify the different emotions that we may experience depending on what we are thinking.
To reframe a range of pictures so that positive and negative feelings are created.

Positive thinking

KS1/2/3

1. Divide the children into groups. Give the groups sets of the box people pictures and ask them to come up with a negative thought about the picture and then the emotion it might lead to, e.g. the box person who is stuck in the mud might think 'Oh no he's never going to get me out.' This might then lead to fear.

2. Write the negative thoughts in the thought bubbles in red pen.

3. Once the groups have found negative thoughts for each picture, ask them to now work together to come up with positive thoughts for each picture, e.g. the box person who is stuck in the mud might think 'Brilliant he's got a rope, I will soon be out of here.' This thought might lead to a happy emotion.

4. Ask the children to write these thoughts in the thought bubbles in green pen.

5. Share all the ideas that the children have created.

6. If a child grows up in a family where the experience is of people solving problems and enjoying the challenges life sends them, what sort of thinking is likely to be created? Pose the question to the children: 'What sort of classroom do we want to create together?' List the types of ways that the class would like to be or respond to each other.

KS2/3

1. Ask children to find some pictures of their own and place them on the thinking circle.

2. Ask them to show how the thinking can be turned from negative to positive and how this will then impact on the person's emotion.

3. How can this skill of reframing be stretched and strengthened?

RESOURCES

1. Box People pictures

2. Laminated speech bubbles

3. Plain paper and pens

4. Thinking Circle

5. Felt pens and markers

Positive thinking

IMPORTANT POINTS

Problem solving skills can be developed with practice.

Positive self-talk is a useful skill to develop.

LEARNING LINKS

Speaking and listening, collaboration, information processing, questioning, observation, creativity, planning and organisation, teamwork.

REFLECTION

Questions:

Positive comment from child:

Positive comment from adult:

LEARNING DIMENSIONS		SOCIAL & EMOTIONAL SKILLS	
Strategic awareness	🟧	Emotional literacy	🟩
Learning relationships		Neuroscience	
Curiosity	🟧	Self-regulation	
Creativity	🟧	Self-development	🟩
Meaning making	🟧		
Changing & learning	🟧		
Resilience	🟩		

Positive thinking

Positive thinking

Positive thinking

Positive thinking

THINKING CIRCLE

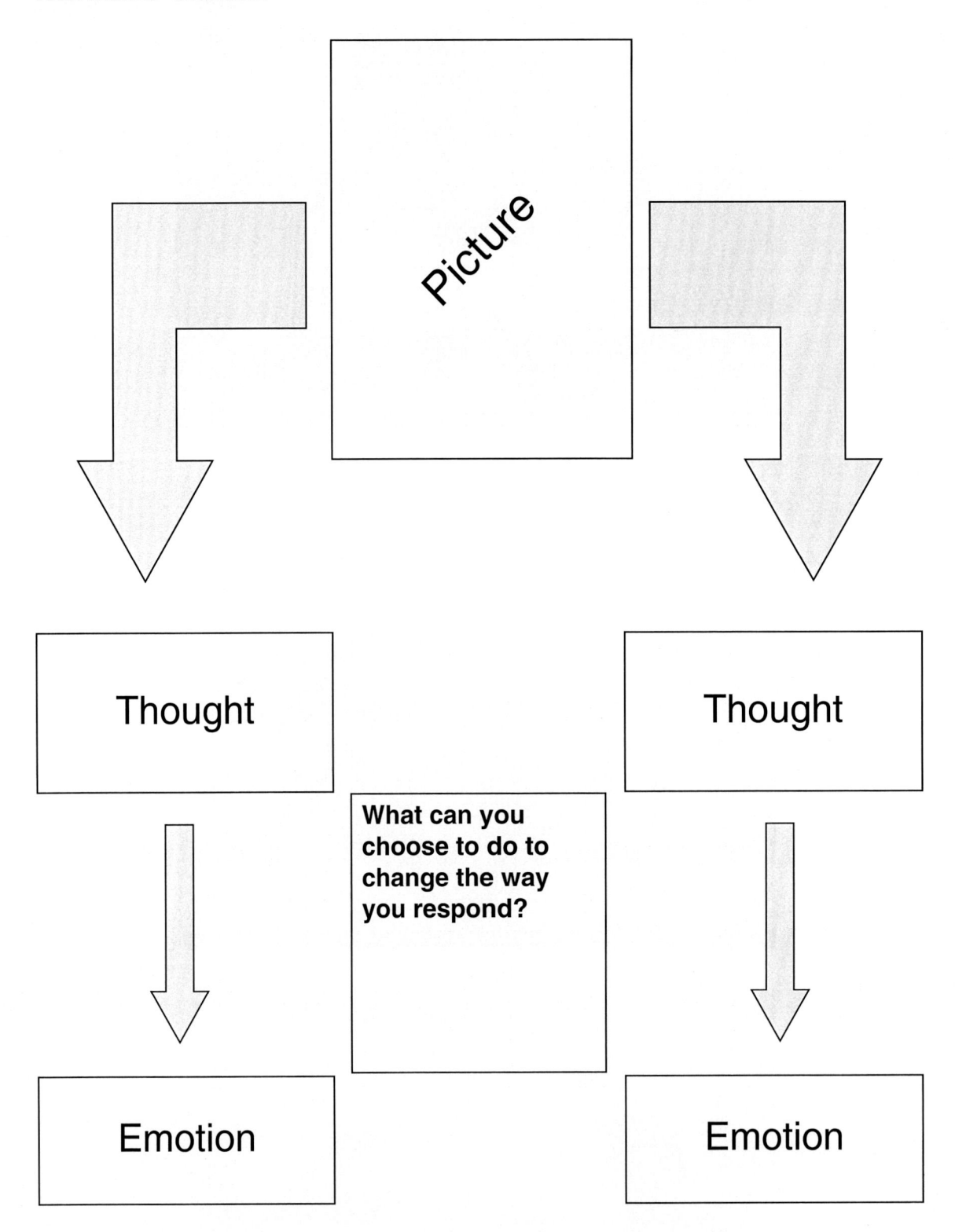

Picture

Thought

Thought

What can you choose to do to change the way you respond?

Emotion

Emotion

Positive thinking

Positive thinking

The best mistake I ever made!

SESSION OBJECTIVES

To enable children to explore the benefits of mistakes.

To enable children to celebrate mistakes and identify what they gained from making them.

SESSION OUTCOMES

✓ To understand the learning opportunities that a mistake can give.

LESSON PLAN

➢ Ask the children to think about their class baby and identify a time when they got something wrong. Ask the children to think about what that enabled the baby/toddler to then go on and do.

➢ Ask the children what they think it must be like to be a parent – How do you know what to do? Explore whether they think parents make mistakes.

For those classrooms not able to undertake the Circles for Learning Project, video clips or photographs can be used to support the discussion around the topic and stimulate thoughts and ideas from the children and young people.

Task

KS1: To draw a picture or share 'My Best Mistake Ever' and explain what they learnt from it.
KS2/3: To create a gallery of mistakes showing mistakes that had been made and what the children/young people/adults got out of them.

1. Show the children a picture of a bottle of medicine. Share the story of how penicillin was found. Fleming left the top off the Petri dish and discovered mould for the first time. The mould was penicillin.

Positive thinking

2. Share a picture of the Leaning Tower of Pisa. Talk about how the architect and builder must have felt. Explore with the children what they might have learnt and taken into the future with them.

KS1/2

Ask the children to draw a picture of their best ever mistake. Ask them to share with each other and talk about what they learnt.

KS2/3

1. Put the children into pairs. Ask them to share a mistake they have made. How did they feel? What did they do to manage this feeling? What was the self-talk that they used?

2. Share these together and compile a list of feelings experienced when making mistakes. Compile a list of ways of managing these feelings. Ask the children what the learning was that developed from the mistake. List the learning alongside each of the mistakes shared.

3. Create a board for 'Best Mistake of the Week'. Ask visiting teachers to contribute. Ask teachers to send in their best mistake and what they took from them and play Room 101.

RESOURCES

1. Sticky notes

2. Plain paper and pens

3. Photographs of mistakes: Leaning Tower of Pisa, penicillin, Christopher Columbus, the Titanic

IMPORTANT POINTS

Mistakes are important in the learning process. Learning how to manage and cope with them is important in developing resilience.

LEARNING LINKS

Speaking and listening, collaboration, information processing, questioning, observation, creativity, planning and organisation, teamwork.

REFLECTION

Questions:

Positive thinking

....

    Positive comment from child:

    Positive comment from adult:

LEARNING DIMENSIONS		SOCIAL & EMOTIONAL SKILLS	
Strategic awareness	🟧	Emotional literacy	🟩
Learning relationships		Neuroscience	
Curiosity	🟧	Self-regulation	
Creativity	🟧	Self-development	🟩
Meaning making	🟧		
Changing & learning	🟧		
Resilience	🟩		

Positive thinking

Rose-tinted glasses

SESSION OBJECTIVES

To explore the link between what we think and how it makes us feel.

SESSION OUTCOMES

✓ To be able to see things in a more positive way.

✓ To be able to change our negative thinking to more positive thinking.

LESSON PLAN

➢ Ask the children to think about their class baby and identify a time when they heard the parent talk about something their class baby had done in a positive way.

➢ How do they think the parent interprets the actions and behaviour of the baby when they have been up all night with them?

➢ How do you think they interpret the actions and behaviour of the class baby when they have had a lovely day with them?

➢ How important is their interpretation to the baby?

For those classrooms not able to undertake the Circles for Learning Project, video clips or photographs can be used to support the discussion around the topic and stimulate thoughts and ideas from the children and young people.

Task

KS1: To create a pair of rose-tinted glasses and a pair of grey-tinted glasses.
KS2/3: To write a young person's report from a positive view and a negative view.

KS1

1. Share some pictures with the children and ask them to describe what has happened. Support them making the link between seeing something in a negative way and how we feel and seeing something in a positive way and the way that makes us feel.

Positive thinking

2. Share the phrase rose-coloured glasses with the children.

3. Ask the children to make rose-tinted glasses and grey- tinted glasses and then look at a range of things through each pair of glasses.

4. Help the children make the link between seeing the positive and feeling more positive and seeing the negative and feeling more negative.

5. Pose the question, if we see things in a more positive way, we feel more positive so if we feel more positive, do we see things in a more positive way?

6. Share the glasses in class when undertaking shared marking or giving feedback on another person's work, following up on behaviour or activities.

7. As a class teacher, play with the different glasses. Ask the children which ones they would like you to wear at different times and role play how differently you can see things. Have some fun together.

KS2/3

1. Share the pictures with the children and explore how they see them – negatively or positively.

2. Help the young people make the link between how we feel and how we interpret the world and how we interpret the world and how we feel.

3. Introduce the concept of the rose-tinted glasses.

4. Ask the young people to write a report on Toby (the story of the worst day at school) whilst wearing rose-tinted glasses and then from the point of view of someone wearing grey-tinted glasses.

5. Share the work and discuss how it makes them feel. How did they get into character?

6. What are the strategies that they use to change state?

7. Share and discuss how we can change state.

RESOURCES

1. Sticky notes

2. Plain paper and pens

3. Glasses template

Positive thinking

4. Thoughts, Feelings, Actions Triangle

5. 'My Worst Day' story

6. Pictures showing negative actions or behaviour or disasters.

7. Pictures showing lovely things.

IMPORTANT POINTS

We can change our state of feeling by the thoughts we think.

We can change the way we see the world by the way we feel.

LEARNING LINKS

Speaking and listening, collaboration, information processing, questioning, observation, creativity, planning and organisation, teamwork.

REFLECTION

Questions:

Positive comment from child:

Positive comment from adult:

LEARNING DIMENSIONS		SOCIAL & EMOTIONAL SKILLS	
Strategic awareness	🟧	Emotional literacy	🟩
Learning relationships		Neuroscience	
Curiosity	🟧	Self-regulation	
Creativity	🟧	Self-development	🟩
Meaning making	🟧		
Changing & learning	🟧		
Resilience	🟩		

Copyright material from Alison Waterhouse (2019), *Self-Discovery*, Routledge

Positive thinking

Positive thinking

There is only one person responsible for your happiness

SESSION OBJECTIVES

To explore the relationship between thoughts, feelings and behaviour.

SESSION OUTCOMES

✓ Poster displaying relationship between thoughts, feelings and behaviour.

LESSON PLAN

➢ Ask the children and young people to remember a time when they observed the parent noticing something their class baby had done and commenting on it in a positive way.

➢ Discuss how that felt for the class baby.

➢ Discuss how the parent might see things after they have been up all night with the baby who has had tummy ache or has been sick. Would they be as positive?

For those classrooms not able to undertake the Circles for Learning Project, video clips or photographs can be used to support the discussion around the topic and stimulate thoughts and ideas from the children and young people.

Task

KS1: To create a poster showing ways to be the 'best I can be.'
KS2: To create a poster: 'If you always do what you have always done your will always get what you have always got!'

KS1

1. Share the book *Why Am I Here?* with the children.

2. Discuss and think about ways we can be the best we can be.

3. Ask the children to create a poster showing ways that they can be the best they can be.

Copyright material from Alison Waterhouse (2019), *Self-Discovery*, Routledge

Positive thinking

4. Ask the children to share something they would like to be able to achieve to be the best they can be this term. Write down the targets for each child. Ask each child to share what they may need to be able to achieve these targets. If they need support from other children, ask for a volunteer. Check in with the children at different times and then celebrate when they have achieved what they wanted. As a teacher, it is good to join in too.

KS2

1. Share the story about the artist Alison Lapper with the young people.

2. Discuss.

3. Ask them in pairs to think of 20 reasons not to do their homework. Then to think of five reasons not to make excuses.

4. In pairs ask the children to think of 3 things that are holding them back or preventing them from being successful or happy.

5. Working together, think of things that they could do to make a difference. Try and come up with 5 different strategies for each of the 3 things.

6. Together choose the one strategy that would make a difference.

7. Share the ones you would like with the other members of the class.

    EXAMPLE:
    No money ⟶ Earn some by working or save more pocket money
    My brother always picks on me ⟶ Act differently towards him

8. Make a poster in pairs: 'If you always do what you have always done then you will always get what you have always got.'

RESOURCES

1. Sticky notes

2. Stuff happens + you react = outcome

3. Thoughts, Feelings, Actions Triangle

4. Large paper and felt tip pens

5. Lined paper

6. The book *Why Am I Here?* by Matthew Kelly

Positive thinking

IMPORTANT POINTS

Understand the importance of thoughts, feelings and behaviour and that there is only one person who is responsible for your happiness – **YOU.**

LEARNING LINKS

Speaking and listening, emotional literacy, thoughts, feelings, actions.

REFLECTION

Questions:

Positive comment from child:

Positive comment from adult:

LEARNING DIMENSIONS		SOCIAL & EMOTIONAL SKILLS	
Strategic awareness		Emotional literacy	
Learning relationships		Neuroscience	
Curiosity		Self-regulation	
Creativity		Self-development	
Meaning making			
Changing & learning			
Resilience			

Positive thinking

THERE IS ONLY ONE PERSON WHO IS RESPONSIBLE FOR YOUR HAPPINESS – YOU

TAKE RESPONSIBILITY FOR YOURSELF

Once there was a girl called Alison, who was born with no arms and no legs. This was caused by drugs that her mother had been given by the doctor to prevent her morning sickness when she was pregnant. Alison had hands which were attached to her torso. On the same day that Alison was born a baby boy was born into a very wealthy, caring family.

Alison grew up and became a very famous artist, campaigning for the rights of disabled people. She inspired another artist Marc Quinn who created a giant sculpture of her in Trafalgar Square in London to celebrate what she stood for.

The boy went to the best schools but became de-motivated and involved in crime in his teenage years. He died before his 25th birthday leaving his family devastated by the waste of life.

Why do some people have everything and yet lose it?

Or more importantly, how do some people who have huge obstacles to overcome manage to do so?

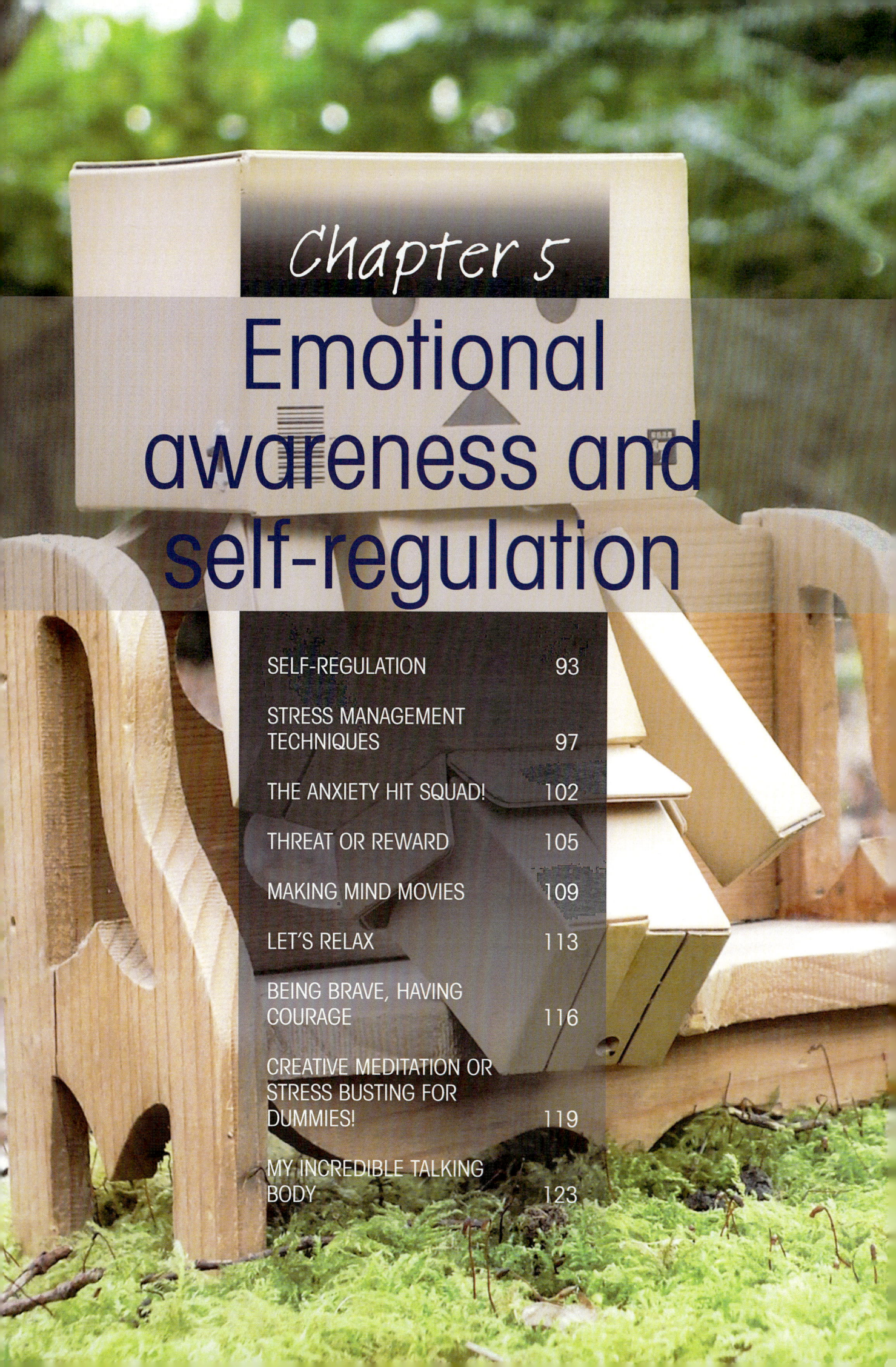

Chapter 5
Emotional awareness and self-regulation

SELF-REGULATION	93
STRESS MANAGEMENT TECHNIQUES	97
THE ANXIETY HIT SQUAD!	102
THREAT OR REWARD	105
MAKING MIND MOVIES	109
LET'S RELAX	113
BEING BRAVE, HAVING COURAGE	116
CREATIVE MEDITATION OR STRESS BUSTING FOR DUMMIES!	119
MY INCREDIBLE TALKING BODY	123

Emotional awareness and self-regulation

Self-regulation

SESSION OBJECTIVES

To explore how we learn to self-regulate and describe how the class baby is supported in doing this.

To explore how we can develop our own ability to self-regulate and share strategies with each other.

SESSION OUTCOMES

- ✓ To create an emotions thermometer to show the different strengths of our emotions.
- ✓ To share and discuss strategies that help us regulate ourselves.
- ✓ To identify both healthy and non-healthy strategies we may use.

LESSON PLAN

- ➤ Ask the children to think about their class baby and identify a time when they were unsettled, upset, cross or frustrated.
- ➤ Ask the children to describe what they saw that told them how the baby was feeling. How did the baby behave and what did that tell them?
- ➤ Discuss how the parent soothed the baby and why or how the baby soothed themselves.

For those classrooms not able to undertake the Circles for Learning Project, video clips or photographs can be used to support the discussion around the topic and stimulate thoughts and ideas from the children and young people.

Task

KS1/2: To create an emotional thermometer to show the strength of their feeling.
    To be able to describe how their body feels when they experience this emotion.
    To be able to identify strategies that help them when they are feeling like this.

KS3: To be able to describe how their body feels when they are experiencing a strong emotion.
    To identify strategies that allow them to manage their feelings and emotions.
    To be able to discuss strategies that people use to self-regulate and to be able to differentiate between those that are healthy and non-healthy.

Copyright material from Alison Waterhouse (2019), *Self-Discovery*, Routledge

Emotional awareness and self-regulation

KS1

1. Share the story of 'Goldilocks and the Three Bears'. Ask the children to imagine how Baby bear felt when he got home and found his porridge eaten, his chair broken and his bed being slept in.

2. Working with the children, list as many words as possible that mean angry - cross, angry, mad etc.

3. Divide the children into groups and ask them to lay out the words with the strongest at the top and the weakest at the bottom.

4. Ask the groups to share their order of words and discuss as a class.

5. On the thermometer put the words down the side to show the intensity of the emotion.

6. Divide the class into pairs and ask them to share ways that they use to calm themselves down.

KS2/3

1. Watch the Harry Potter and Ron argument scene, https://www.youtube.com/watch?v=9_wj_Ml4gSE (accessed 6 November 2018).

2. Discuss how anger can make our bodies feel.

    - Ask children to share where they feel anger first. Which part of their body is their early warning system? Hands, feet, head? Get them to describe what this is like – does it have a colour? A form? If it were an animal what would it be? When they need to tame it what could they use?

3. Working in small groups, identify strategies that help to regulate them when they are angry, e.g. going for a run, counting to 10, breathing in and out 5 times, kicking a football, listening to music, playing video games etc.

4. What about when they feel sad?

5. Ask the children to put together their top 3 strategies for either sad or angry and say why they have chosen them. Get them to think about two aspects : How do they help them regulate? Do they help solve or improve the situation?

6. Ask the children to create their own thermometer and show which strategies work to calm them from 10–7, from 7–4 and from 4–1. Share these together. Ask children to identify a strategy that they haven't tried before which they think they might find useful.

7. For KS3, combine all the suggestions from the class – you may want to talk about alcohol, comfort eating and drugs as ways people use to soothe when they become upset. This enables you to help young people understand that some things are healthy and some are unhealthy for us.

8. Share the impact of visualisation and mindfulness as strategies used by people. This can form the follow-up lesson.

Emotional awareness and self-regulation

RESOURCES

1. Sticky notes
2. Plain paper and pens
3. Thermometer
4. The story of 'Goldilocks and the Three Bears'
5. Art work that shows anger

IMPORTANT POINTS

We all experience strong emotions that make us feel overwhelmed. We can use a range of strategies to help us learn to manage these.

LEARNING LINKS

Speaking and listening, collaboration, information processing, questioning, observation, creativity, planning and organisation, teamwork.

REFLECTION

Questions:

Positive comment from child:

Positive comment from adult:

LEARNING DIMENSIONS		SOCIAL & EMOTIONAL SKILLS	
Strategic awareness		Emotional literacy	green
Learning relationships	orange	Neuroscience	
Curiosity		Self-regulation	
Creativity	orange	Self-development	green
Meaning making	orange		
Changing & learning	orange		
Resilience	green		

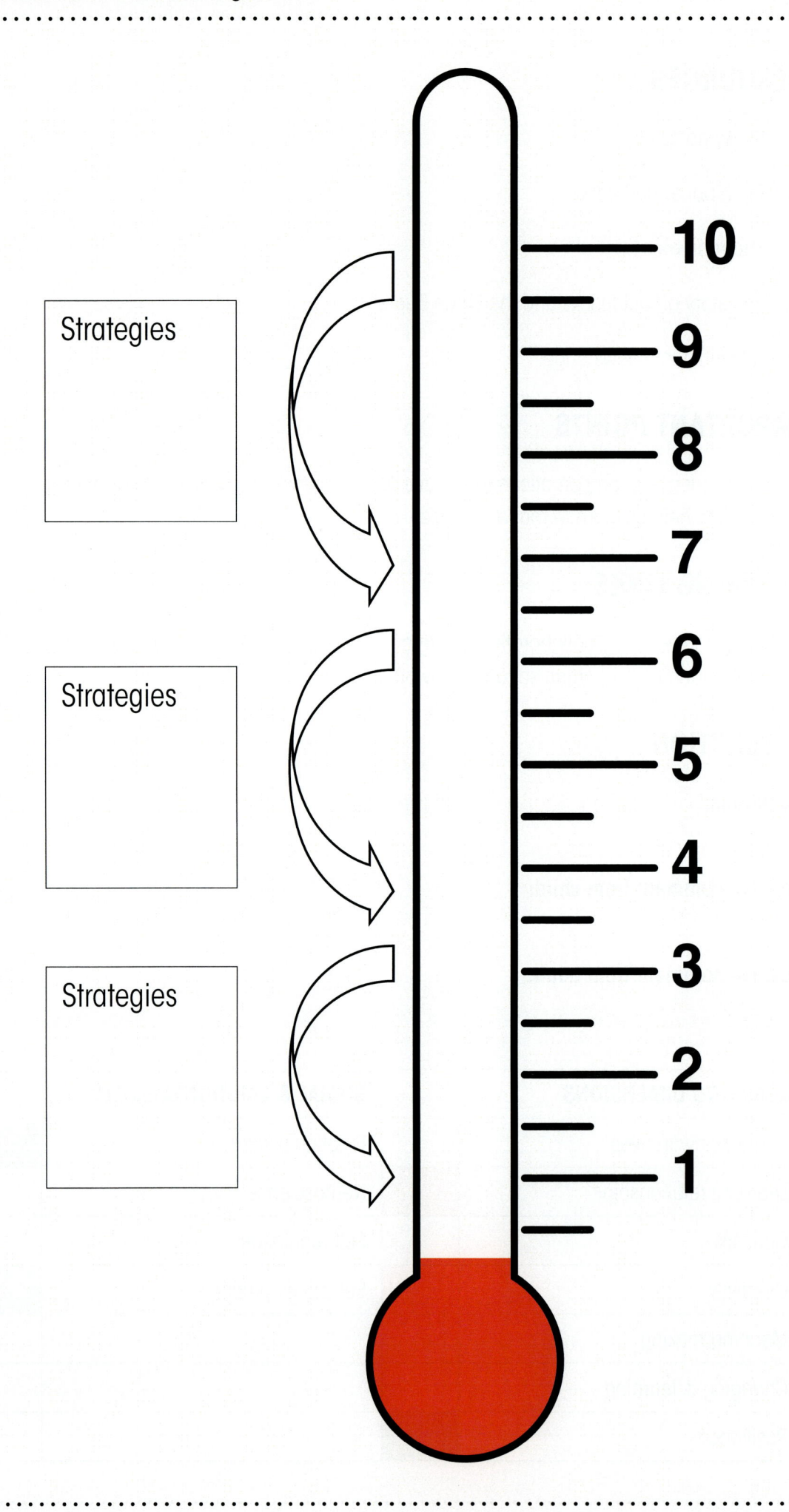

Emotional awareness and self-regulation

Strategies		10
		9
		8
		7
Strategies		6
		5
		4
Strategies		3
		2
		1

Emotional awareness and self-regulation

Stress management techniques

SESSION OBJECTIVES

To be able to identify stress in ourselves and manage this through developing a range of stress management techniques.

SESSION OUTCOMES

✓ Leaflet or poster of stress-busting strategies.

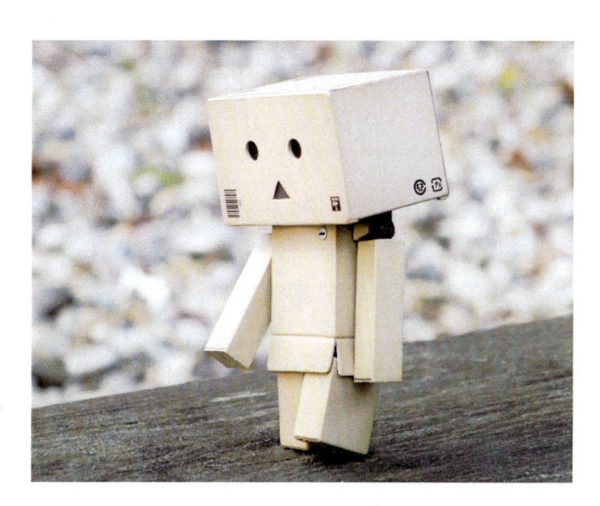

LESSON PLAN

➢ Remind the class of times when their class baby has been overwhelmed and has not been able to cope. Discuss what has happened to cause this and how they might feel.

➢ Identify strategies that helped the baby.

For those classrooms not able to undertake the Circles for Learning Project, video clips or photographs can be used to support the discussion around the topic and stimulate thoughts and ideas from the children and young people.

Task

KS2: What happens in the brain?
    How does stress make us feel?
    Strategies to help us calm and relax.
    Relaxation.

KS3: What happens in the brain?
    How does stress make us feel?
    Strategies to help us calm and relax.
    Stress Room 101.
    Poster or leaflet to show a range of strategies to combat stress.

1. Discuss in pairs: What is stress? Is it good or bad? Do we need it? What purpose does it serve?

2. In pairs or small groups, talk about a time when you were stressed and describe how it felt. List what happens to our mind and bodies when we become stressed.

Emotional awareness and self-regulation

3. Recap on the amygdala and its function. Share the hand model of the brain, https://www.youtube.com/watch?v=f-m2YcdMdFw
   Discuss what happens in the brain.

4. Discuss in pairs 3 things that you find stressful.

5. Introduce a relaxation exercise.

6. Play Stress Room 101. Each person can nominate a 'stressful' thing which they would like to be put into Room 101. At the end the class votes on which thing can go into Room 101.

7. In pairs discuss three strategies you have for 'stress busting'

8. Share these with the class.

9. Create a stress busting leaflet or poster to show a range of strategies to combat stress.

RESOURCES

1. Sticky notes

2. Stress pictures

3. Large box labelled Stress Room 101

4. Paper and pens

5. Brain poster and the amygdala flight, fright, freeze responses

6. Relaxation exercise

IMPORTANT POINTS

- Stress is a natural reaction when we feel under threat.

- We can manage our stress in a variety of ways.

- Relaxation helps us manage stress.

LEARNING LINKS

Thoughts, feelings, actions, self-talk, own best friend, relaxation.

Emotional awareness and self-regulation

REFLECTION

Questions:

Positive comment from child:

Positive comment from adult:

LEARNING DIMENSIONS		SOCIAL & EMOTIONAL SKILLS	
Strategic awareness		Emotional literacy	🟩
Learning relationships	🟧	Neuroscience	
Curiosity		Self-regulation	
Creativity	🟧	Self-development	🟩
Meaning making	🟧		
Changing & learning	🟧		
Resilience	🟩		

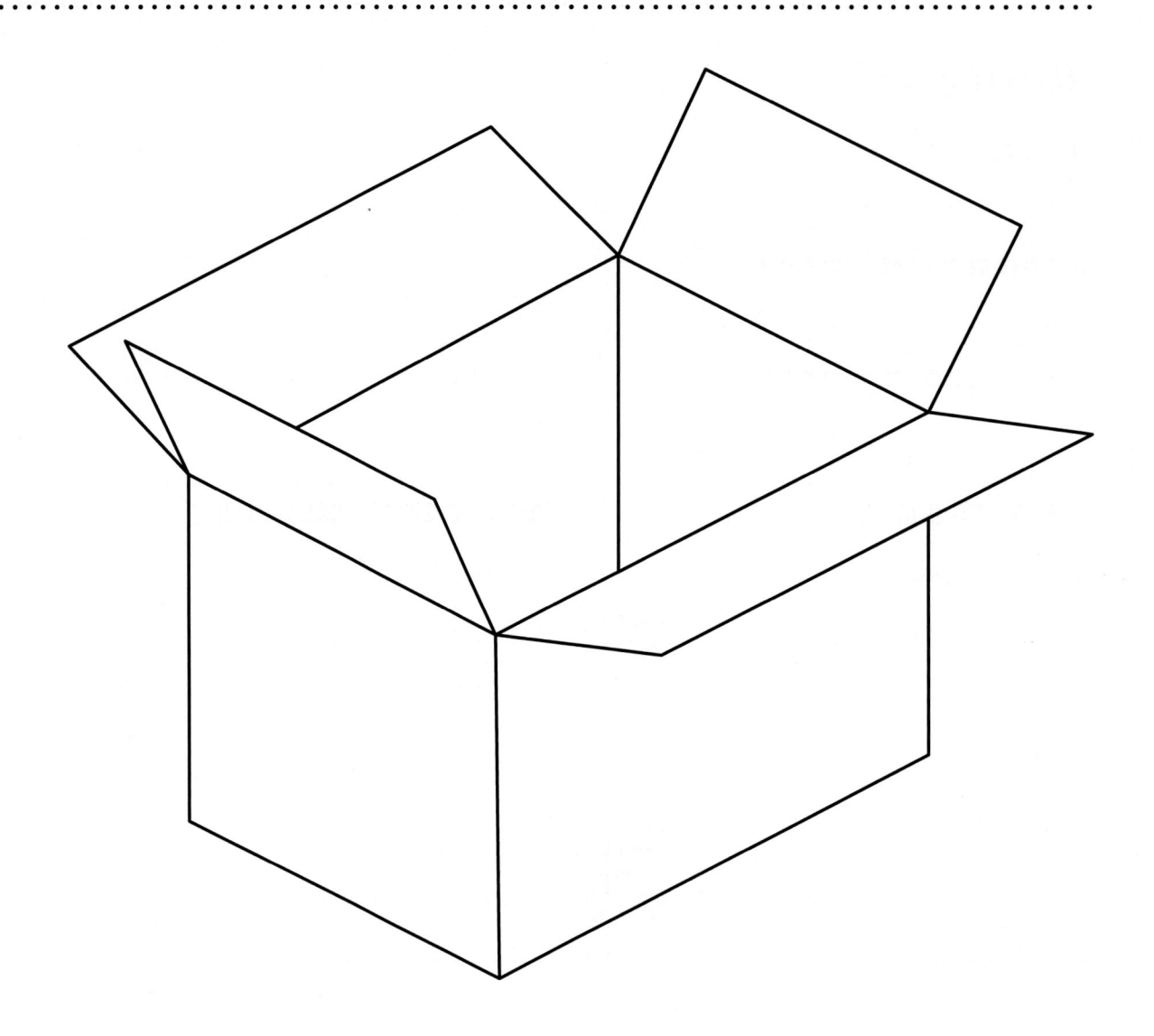

Emotional awareness and self-regulation

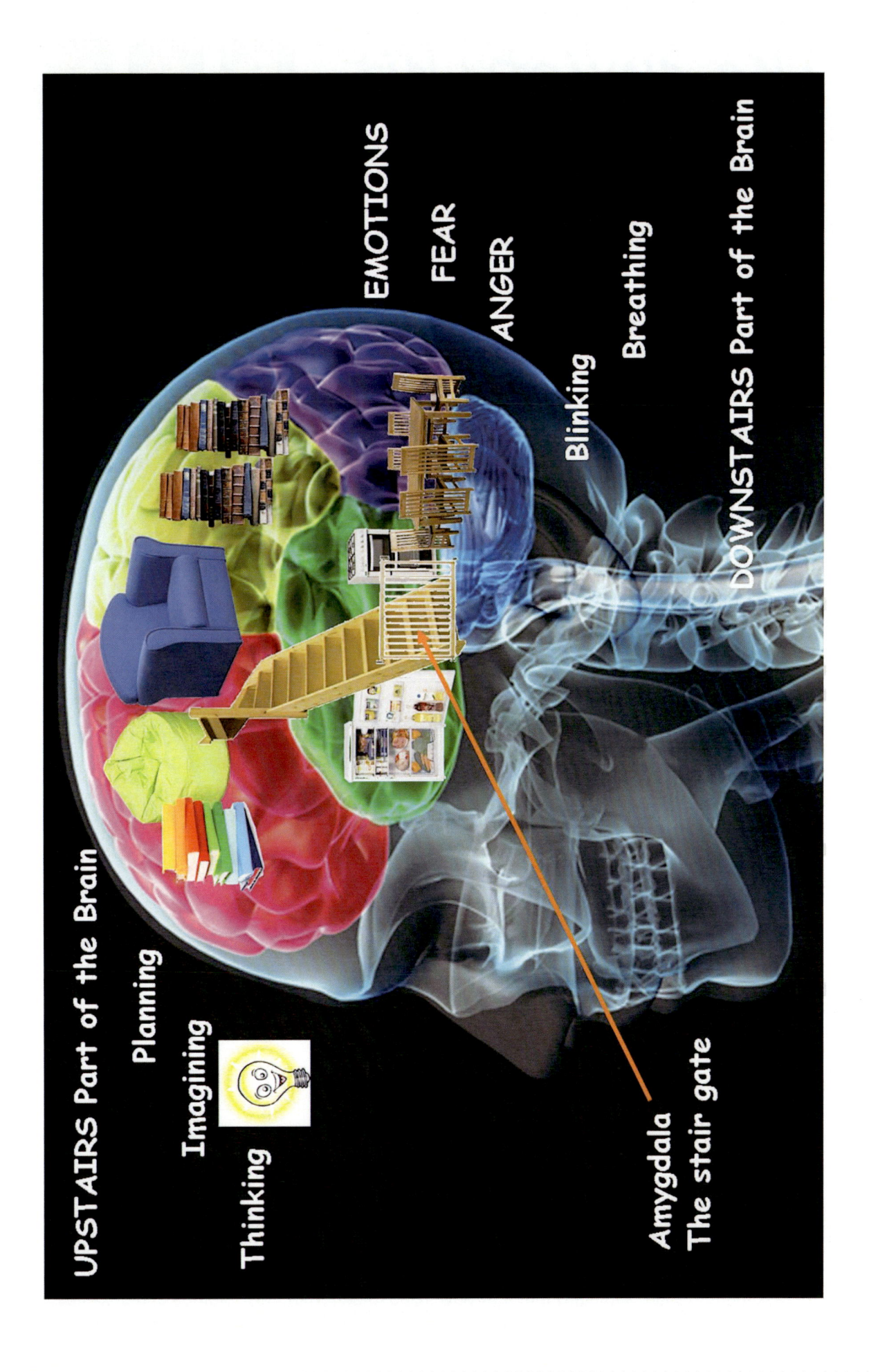

Emotional awareness and self-regulation

101

Emotional awareness and self-regulation

The anxiety hit squad!

SESSION OBJECTIVES

To enable children to explore and identify how worries and anxieties can impact on our lives.

To enable children to explore a range of strategies to deal with worries and anxieties.

SESSION OUTCOMES

- ✓ To identify a range of strategies to deal with worries or anxieties.

LESSON PLAN

- ➤ Ask the children to think about their class baby and identify a time when they sought help or support. Ask the children the ways the baby asked for support – actions and words.

- ➤ Discuss how the parent responded to the request for support. Explore what it must be like to have experienced an adult think about you and respond to your needs. How would that make you think about people and the world that you lived in?

For those classrooms not able to undertake the Circles for Learning Project, video clips or photographs can be used to support the discussion around the topic and stimulate thoughts and ideas from the children and young people.

Task

KS1: To invent a machine or robot that gets rid of worries.
KS2/3: To create a worry/anxiety first aid kit.

KS1

1. Ask the children to think about the different times that they have worried or become anxious over something.

2. Ask them to share strategies that they have used to deal with these worries and anxieties.

Emotional awareness and self-regulation

3. Ask the children to create a robot/draw a robot that can get rid of worries. Ask them to label the different aspects of the robot. These might include a worry tracker, a worry destroyer, a calm injection, resilient spray etc.

KS2/3

1. Ask the children to think about the different times that they have worried or become anxious over something.

2. Ask them to share strategies that they have used to deal with these worries and anxieties.

3. In pairs ask them to create a worry first aid kit. They can be as creative as they like!

4. Share these with the class.

5. Link the ability to manage anxiety and worries with being resilient – managing to deal with different things.

RESOURCES

1. Sticky notes

2. Plain paper and pens

IMPORTANT POINTS

We have people around us who can help if we ask them.

Sometimes it takes courage to ask for help and to accept it.

LEARNING LINKS

Speaking and listening, collaboration, information processing, questioning, observation, creativity, planning and organisation, teamwork.

REFLECTION

Questions:

Positive comment from child:

Positive comment from adult:

Emotional awareness and self-regulation

LEARNING DIMENSIONS		SOCIAL & EMOTIONAL SKILLS	
Strategic awareness	🟧	Emotional literacy	🟩
Learning relationships		Neuroscience	
Curiosity	🟧	Self-regulation	
Creativity	🟧	Self-development	🟩
Meaning making	🟧		
Changing & learning	🟧		
Resilience	🟩		

Emotional awareness and self-regulation

Threat or reward

SESSION OBJECTIVES

To understand how our brain tries to protect us and what happens in our brain to make us experience emotions.

SESSION OUTCOMES

✓ Know which part of our brain is responsible for our emotions – the amygdala.

✓ Know that our brain is trying to protect us and so releases chemicals into our body to help.

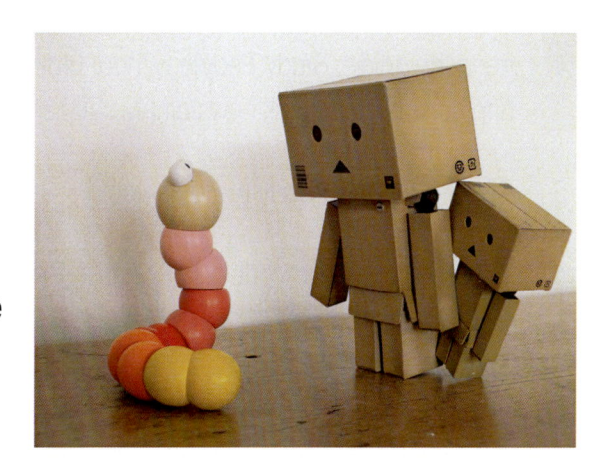

LESSON PLAN

➢ Ask the children to remember a time when they saw their class baby frightened.

➢ Ask them to describe what they observed.

➢ How did the baby calm?

For those classrooms not able to undertake the Circles for Learning Project, video clips or photographs can be used to support the discussion around the topic and stimulate thoughts and ideas from the children and young people.

Task

KS1: To draw a picture showing something they are frightened of.
   To share strategies that they use to help themselves feel less afraid.
KS2/3: To create a cartoon strip to show what happens when the senses send the brain a warning.

KS1

1. Read the story *The Owl Who Was Afraid of the Dark* by Jill Tomlinson.

2. Discuss what it is like to be frightened.

3. Share strategies that can be used to help us when we are frightened.

Copyright material from Alison Waterhouse (2019), *Self-Discovery*, Routledge

105

Emotional awareness and self-regulation

4. Create a picture to show being frightened and then what to do about it.

KS2/3

1. Show *Harry Potter and the Prisoner of Azkaban* – the Dementor attack in the train YouTube clip, https://www.youtube.com/watch?v=NQ6-h2zeBfg (accessed 6 November 2018).

2. Discuss what it feels like to be frightened.

3. Share the brain model with the young people and find the amygdala.

4. Read the article: 'Study: People without brain's "fear centre" can still be scared' (by Ian Steadman), http://www.wired.co.uk/news/archive/2013-02-04/amygdala-brain-fear-centre-mystery

5. Discuss how the body protects itself.

6. Watch 'How the amygdala hijacks the brain', https://www.youtube.com/watch?v=xNY0AAUtH3g.

7. Create a cartoon to show how the brain deals with threats.

8. Share these.

RESOURCES

1. Large flip chart

2. Pens for flip chart

3. Pictures reward or threat

4. Amygdala

5. Brain model

6. Reward or threat cartoon sheet

7. The body's response to threat diagram

8. *The Owl Who Was Afraid of the Dark* by Jill Tomlinson

IMPORTANT POINTS

The **amygdala** is an almond-shaped structure in the brain; its name comes from the Greek word for "almond". As with most other brain structures, you actually have two amygdala. Each amygdala is located close to the hippocampus, in the frontal portion of the temporal lobe.

Emotional awareness and self-regulation

Your amygdala are essential to your ability to feel certain emotions and to perceive them in other people. This includes fear and the many changes that it causes in the body. If you are being followed at night by a suspicious-looking individual and your heart is pounding, the chances are that your amygdala are very active!

Our brain looks for rewards or threats. If it sees a threat it releases chemicals to help us manage that threat. It gets us ready to **Fight, Flight, Freeze or Flock.** The chemicals it releases are cortisol and adrenaline.

If our brain sees a reward – something that we like – it releases serotonin and dopamine. These are the pleasure chemicals.

Our emotional brain will often hijack our thinking brain. Our behaviour can sometimes get us into trouble because of this.

LEARNING LINKS

Speaking and listening, literacy, Science.

REFLECTION

Questions:

Positive comment from child:

Positive comment from adult:

LEARNING DIMENSIONS		SOCIAL & EMOTIONAL SKILLS	
Strategic awareness	🟧	Emotional literacy	🟩
Learning relationships		Neuroscience	
Curiosity	🟧	Self-regulation	
Creativity	🟧	Self-development	🟩
Meaning making	🟧		
Changing & learning	🟧		
Resilience	🟩		

Emotional awareness and self-regulation

Cortisol

Adrenaline

Threat

Dopamine

Serotonin

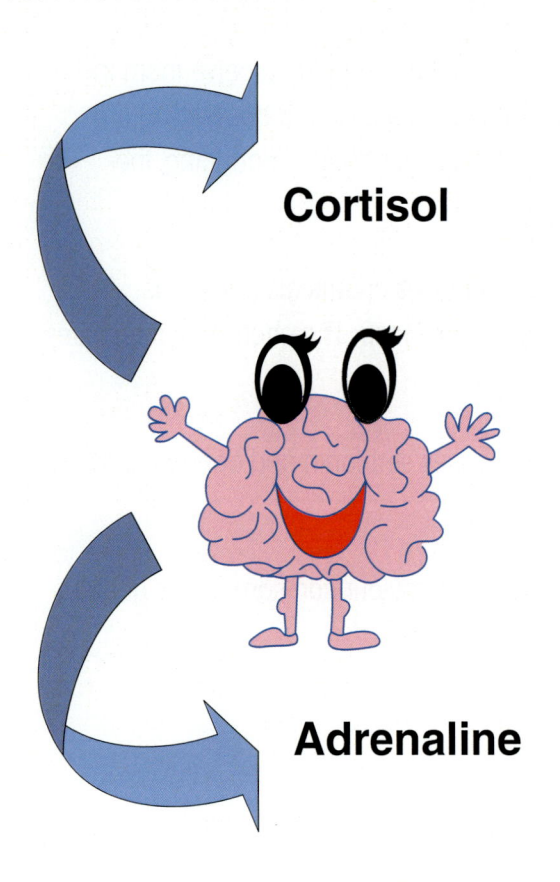

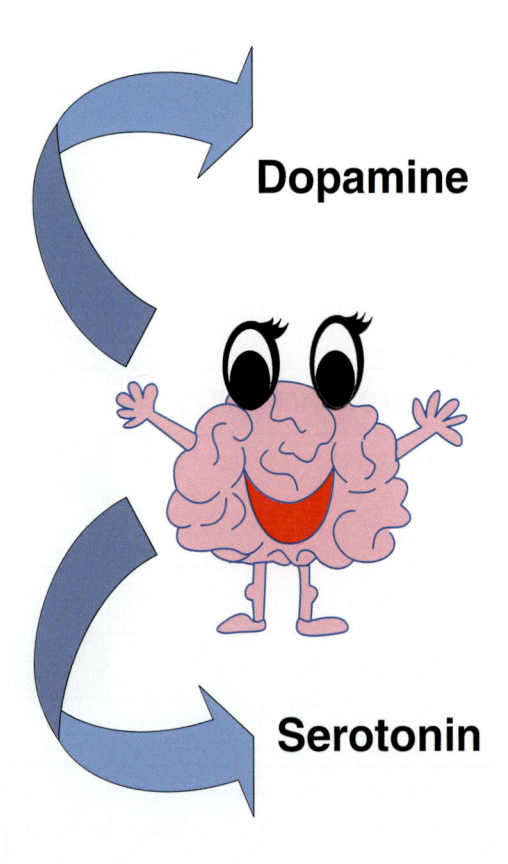

Reward

Emotional awareness and self-regulation

Making mind movies

SESSION OBJECTIVES

To utilise visualisation techniques.

SESSION OUTCOMES

✓ Strengthen own ability to have confidence and self-belief.

✓ Make mind movies to help confidence and self-belief.

LESSON PLAN

➢ Remind the children of a time when their class baby managed to achieve something – walking, crawling, standing up etc. Ask them to think about what the baby had pictured in his/her mind. Had they pictured themselves falling or slipping or had they pictured themselves getting to where they wanted to go?

For those classrooms not able to undertake the Circles for Learning Project, video clips or photographs can be used to support the discussion around the topic and stimulate thoughts and ideas from the children and young people.

Task

KS1: Self-belief seeds.
KS2/3: Self-belief poster.

KS1

1. Show children a seed or bean and ask them what would happen to it if it was put in a pot of soil. Ask them to imagine that it is something that they are learning to do – ride a bike, tell the time etc.

2. Discuss how it will grow but only if it has light and water to keep it going.

3. Ask them what it would need if it was a self-belief bean. A positive environment – kind and thoughtful food – encouraging words.

Emotional awareness and self-regulation

4. Give them the picture of a bean in a pot and ask them to write the supportive words around it that would make it grow.

5. Then ask them to draw the plant at different stages and link this to them achieving what they want to do. A list of stages for an activity or task can be given the children for them to put in the correct order: the stem, with leaves, with a flower.

6. Next time you teach the children something, ask them to show where their Self-esteem Bean is in that area?

7. Use the Self-esteem Bean when working in other areas.

KS2/3

1. Ask children what they picture in their minds eye when they go to do something.

2. Do they see themselves achieving what they want? Or do they see themselves failing?

3. KS2/3 Discuss David Beckam and his curved goal. Show them a video clip of this. David would spend hours imagining himself kicking this shot. He would feel what it was like, he would see himself doing this, he would see it, feel it, and hear it.

4. Introduce Chuckle Knuckles.

5. After doing the activity, ask the young people how they feel now – rate it compared with the beginning of the lesson.

6. Discuss different ways that we can influence our sense of being positive. Examples might be positive music, films, a statement or phrase.

7. Get the children/young people to list songs that make them happy, inspired and confident. Share them and vote for the best.

8. Get the children/young people to draw the picture they visualised with the positive music the class chose in the background. Get them to write on it the phrase they have chosen and the gesture they have decided to use.

9. Use the music during another lesson to test how well it lifts the mood. It will.

RESOURCES

1. Sticky notes

2. Beans

3. Plant picture – stem, with leaves, in flower

Emotional awareness and self-regulation

4. Selection of inspiring music – 'Survivor' by Destiny's Child, 'We Are the Champions' by Queen, 'I Believe I Can Fly' by R. Kelly

5. Selection of positive phrases

6. Plain paper and pens

7. Chuckle Knuckles sheet

IMPORTANT POINTS

If we can see ourselves achieving something, this supports us doing it.

Visualisation can be a very powerful strategy.

LEARNING LINKS

Speaking and listening, collaboration, information processing, questioning, observation, creativity, planning and organisation, teamwork.

REFLECTION

Questions:

Positive comment from child:

Positive comment from adult:

LEARNING DIMENSIONS		SOCIAL & EMOTIONAL SKILLS	
Strategic awareness	🟧	Emotional literacy	🟩
Learning relationships		Neuroscience	
Curiosity	🟧	Self-regulation	
Creativity	🟧	Self-development	🟩
Meaning making	🟧		
Changing & learning	🟧		
Resilience	🟩		

Emotional awareness and self-regulation

CHUCKLE KNUCKLES

Ask the children to sit comfortably and relax.

Ask them to shut their eyes and picture a time when they felt really positive and successful.

Ask them to choose one of those times and see it in their mind's eye. It may have been in a game, a performance, an exam, working with friends, an activity they have achieved outside school. But they need to have felt amazing and really good about themselves.

Ask them to create that time like a movie in their heads. (If they can't think of one then they can make one that they would like.)

Ask them to play that movie in their mind's eye, make the colours bright and vibrant, and the picture clear and big – filling the whole screen turn up the sound. (Allow time for them to achieve this.)

Feel what it felt like to be that successful, see what you could see, hear what you could hear, as everyone tells you how fantastic you have been.

Keep that feeling going.

Tell them that you are going to turn on the music you have chosen and ask them to add this to their movie as the soundtrack. Tell them you want them to make a physical gesture such as a fist pump that goes with their internal movie. When they have done this, ask them to see themselves making the gesture and then adding a phrase such as 'Go for it' or 'You can do this'.

See it, hear it, feel it, be it. Ask the children to press their knuckles as the feeling reaches its peak, press and count to eight.

Emotional awareness and self-regulation

Let's relax

SESSION OBJECTIVES

To learn that the brain and body both need regular, focused down- time to be able to work and learn effectively.

SESSION OUTCOMES

- ✓ A five-step plan to relax.
- ✓ Experience relaxation.

LESSON PLAN

- ➢ Ask the children to remember how their baby relaxes. What do they need/want?
- ➢ Think of different times that they have observed their baby in different states – full of energy, relaxed and chilled, stress, tetchy etc.

For those classrooms not able to undertake the Circles for Learning Project, video clips or photographs can be used to support the discussion around the topic and stimulate thoughts and ideas from the children and young people.

Task

KS1: To be able to draw a picture of themselves experiencing different states.
KS2/3: To be able to create a poster to show 5 steps to relaxation.

KS1

1. Put the children into small groups. Show children different pictures of children doing different things. Ask them to put the pictures into groups: calm, excited, focused.

2. Ask the children to put the different scents (from the collection of scented objects) into the different groups.

3. Ask the children to put the music into the different groups.

4. Discuss the different states we feel during a day.

5. Ask children to think about how they cope with getting from one state to another.

6. Explore strategies that they use.

Copyright material from Alison Waterhouse (2019), *Self-Discovery*, Routledge

113

Emotional awareness and self-regulation

7. Think about bed-time and how they get to sleep.

8. Draw a picture of themselves in 3 different states.

KS2/3

1. Working in teams, ask the children to link the words and pictures and smells.

    - Relaxed
    - Exhilarated
    - Focused

2. Share the learning graph with the children and discuss where they do their best learning.

3. Ask them to share how they get from one stage to another – what strategies do they use?

    Excited to Focused
    Focused to Calm
    Calm to Focused
    Focused to Excited

4. Put the children in teams – the challenge is to create a 5-step guide to relaxation poster.

5. Go through the success criteria that make a good poster together:

    - The poster needs to contain 5 steps.
    - There should be appropriate music playing throughout.
    - It should help people to feel relaxed.

6. After completion, get the class to assess each contribution against the success criteria.

7. Share a visualisation piece with the children.

RESOURCES

1. Large flip chart
2. Pens for flip chart
3. Sticky notes
4. Paper and pens
5. Coloured pens
6. Computer access

Emotional awareness and self-regulation

7. Selection of magazines and holiday brochures

8. Lavender, lemon, mint, coffee, vanilla, basil scents or objects

9. Selection of music to show calm and relaxed, excited and focused

10. Pictures of children doing a range of activities

11. Visualisation piece

IMPORTANT POINTS

- Steps to relaxation.
- Working together.

LEARNING LINKS

Speaking and listening, collaboration, information processing, questioning, observation, creativity, planning and organisation.

REFLECTION

Questions:

Positive comment from child:

Positive comment from adult:

LEARNING DIMENSIONS		SOCIAL & EMOTIONAL SKILLS	
Strategic awareness	🟧	Emotional literacy	🟩
Learning relationships		Neuroscience	
Curiosity	🟧	Self-regulation	
Creativity	🟧	Self-development	🟩
Meaning making	🟧		
Changing & learning	🟧		
Resilience	🟩		

Emotional awareness and self-regulation

Being brave, having courage

SESSION OBJECTIVES

To explore what it is like to be brave.

To explore how we can develop the ability to be courageous.

SESSION OUTCOMES

✓ To identify role models who show bravery.

✓ To explore bravery in many different forms.

✓ To create a super-hero who celebrates bravery and helps people to be more courageous.

LESSON PLAN

➢ Ask the children to think about their class baby and identify a time when they demonstrated being brave or courageous.

➢ Explore what enabled the baby to act in this way.

➢ Watch the video clip of the baby crawling over Perspex. The Visual Cliff Experiment, https://www.youtube.com/watch?v=p6cqNhHrMJA

➢ Discuss with the children how the baby felt. How did they know? What enabled the baby to keep going even when they sensed danger?

For those classrooms not able to undertake the Circles for Learning Project, video clips or photographs can be used to support the discussion around the topic and stimulate thoughts and ideas from the children and young people.

Task

KS1: To explore characters from stories who show bravery.
  Draw a picture of themselves being brave.
KS2/3: To explore role models and real-life stories of people who have demonstrated bravery and courage.

Emotional awareness and self-regulation

To create a cartoon super-hero who gives people a range of things to make them brave or courageous.

KS1

1. Share a fairy story. Ask the children to identify who was brave. Discuss what they did and how they may have felt.

2. Ask the children to share a time when they were brave – going to the hospital, doctor or dentist, flying in an aeroplane, holding a spider, stroking a dog.

3. Share the fact that we are all afraid of different things.

4. Explore why fear is a good thing and how it can help us.

5. Share how we can manage fear – this is being brave and courageous.

6. Draw a picture of a time when they were brave. Ask the children to show the positive self-talk that helped them.

7. Read the book *You Can Do It, Bert* by Ole Könnecke. Link to being brave making us more resilient.

KS2/3

1. Share pictures of famous people who have been brave or done extraordinary things.

2. Explore what this may have been like, their feelings, how it felt to conquer being afraid, what it felt like when they achieved this.

3. Ask the children to share a time when they had to be brave or courageous. Explore what enabled them to do this.

4. Ask the children to create a comic book super-hero. Create their backpack of equipment. What would it contain? Positive self-talk spray, nerves of steel tablets, positive belief bracelet etc.

RESOURCES

1. Sticky notes

2. Plain paper and pens

3. *You Can Do It, Bert* by Ole Könnecke

4. Photographs of famous people who have shown bravery and courage.

5. Fairy tales: 'Little Red Riding Hood', 'Jack and the Beanstalk', 'Hansel and Gretel'

6. Pictures of comic heroes

Emotional awareness and self-regulation

IMPORTANT POINTS

We have all been courageous at different times and with different things.

We can use a range of strategies when we need to be brave.

LEARNING LINKS

Speaking and listening, collaboration, information processing, questioning, observation, creativity, planning and organisation, teamwork.

REFLECTION

Questions:

Positive comment from child:

Positive comment from adult:

LEARNING DIMENSIONS		SOCIAL & EMOTIONAL SKILLS	
Strategic awareness	🟧	Emotional literacy	🟩
Learning relationships		Neuroscience	
Curiosity	🟧	Self-regulation	
Creativity	🟧	Self-development	🟩
Meaning making	🟧		
Changing & learning	🟧		
Resilience	🟩		

Emotional awareness and self-regulation

Creative meditation or stress busting for dummies!

SESSION OBJECTIVES

To learn that the brain and body both need regular, focused down-time to be able to work and learn effectively.

SESSION OUTCOMES

- ✓ A 'ten steps to relax and refresh' poster or PowerPoint.

- ✓ Experience relaxation.

LESSON PLAN

- ➢ Ask the children to remember a time when their class baby was very excitable. How did the parent calm them?

- ➢ What sort of emotional state did their class baby need to be in to be able to learn?

For those classrooms not able to undertake the Circles for Learning Project, video clips or photographs can be used to support the discussion around the topic and stimulate thoughts and ideas from the children and young people.

Task
KS1: To be able to share ways that they use to get themselves into the learning zone.
KS2: To create a relaxing PowerPoint.

KS1
1. Remind the children about the different states that they can experience – calm, focused, excited, etc.

2. Discuss which state is better for learning.

Emotional awareness and self-regulation

3. Discuss how the children get themselves into a learning state.

4. Create a class poster to show 'How we get ourselves ready for learning'.

KS2

1. Show the children a range of pictures and ask them to choose the most relaxing ones.

2. Play a range of music and ask them to choose the most restful pieces.

3. Remind the children of the arousal curve and the best learning zone area.

4. Discuss visualisation and relaxation and explain why it is important for the brain to rest and recharge and to calm when too excited or experiencing a high emotion.

5. Ask the question 'How good would it be if you were in charge of your own energiser?'

6. Ask the children to design a PowerPoint that enables the viewer to relax and calm to de-stress.

7. Discuss the success criteria and agree and then test out the PowerPoints against these criteria when they have been completed.

8. Share a visualisation with them and discuss the metaphor of an internal journey to a place of calm and peace.

RESOURCES

1. Large flip chart

2. Pens for flip chart

3. Sticky notes

4. Paper and pens

5. Coloured pens

6. Computer access

7. Music

8. Arousal zone picture

Emotional awareness and self-regulation

IMPORTANT POINTS

- Steps to relaxation.
- Working together.

LEARNING LINKS

Speaking and listening, collaboration, information processing, questioning, observation, creativity, planning and organisation.

REFLECTION

Questions:

Positive comment from child:

Positive comment from adult:

LEARNING DIMENSIONS		SOCIAL & EMOTIONAL SKILLS	
Strategic awareness	🟧	Emotional literacy	🟩
Learning relationships		Neuroscience	
Curiosity	🟧	Self-regulation	
Creativity	🟧	Self-development	🟩
Meaning making	🟧		
Changing & learning	🟧		
Resilience	🟩		

Emotional awareness and self-regulation

Arousal zones

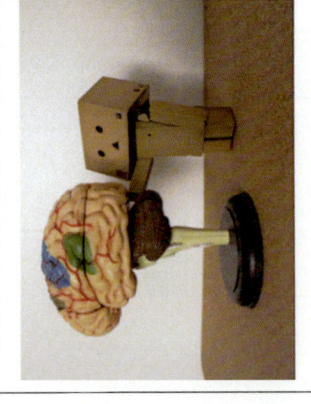

Over Active Zone Hyperactive

Optimal Learning Zone

Under Active Zone Hypoactive

ENERGY LEVELS

TIME

122 — Copyright material from Alison Waterhouse (2019), *Self-Discovery*, Routledge

Emotional awareness and self-regulation

My incredible talking body

SESSION OBJECTIVES

To learn that the body can become an early warning system.

SESSION OUTCOMES

- ✓ An ability to listen to our bodies.
- ✓ Experience relaxation.

LESSON PLAN

➢ Ask the children to remember a time when their class parent helped their baby to understand how he/she felt by telling them that they were . . .

➢ Ask the children to think about how they learnt what different feelings felt like.

➢ Do they all feel the same when they are excited or sad?

For those classrooms not able to undertake the Circles for Learning Project, video clips or photographs can be used to support the discussion around the topic and stimulate thoughts and ideas from the children and young people.

Task

KS1: To enable the children to listen to their bodies.
KS2: To create a picture that they can visualise if they need to calm or feel happy or safe.

KS1/KS2

1. Remind the children about the different states that they can experience – calm, angry, sad, excited etc.

2. Read the story *My Incredible Talking Body* by Rebecca Bowen.

3. If they could ask a question to one of the characters in the story what would it be?

4. Ask the children to draw a picture of a pretend holiday. The holiday scene needs to be perfect and make them feel happy, relaxed and calm.

Emotional awareness and self-regulation

5. Discuss what it needs to show – where it is, who is there, what they are doing, how it makes them feel.

6. Ask the children to share with the group why they chose the place they chose.

7. Put the picture up around the class so that the children can easily see their own. Make small versions for them to have in their drawer.

8. Get the children to use the pictures as a way of calming at different times of the day – let's go on holiday for a minute!

RESOURCES

1. Large flip chart
2. Pens for flip chart
3. Sticky notes
4. Paper and pens
5. Coloured pens
6. Holiday brochures
7. *My Incredible Talking Body* by Rebecca Bowen

IMPORTANT POINTS

- Steps to relaxation.
- Working together.

LEARNING LINKS

Speaking and listening, collaboration, information processing, questioning, observation, creativity, planning and organisation.

REFLECTION

Questions:

Emotional awareness and self-regulation

Positive comment from child:

Positive comment from adult:

LEARNING DIMENSIONS		SOCIAL & EMOTIONAL SKILLS	
Strategic awareness	🟧	Emotional literacy	🟩
Learning relationships		Neuroscience	
Curiosity	🟧	Self-regulation	
Creativity	🟧	Self-development	🟩
Meaning making	🟧		
Changing & learning	🟧		
Resilience	🟩		

Chapter 6
Empathy

WALKING IN ANOTHER PERSON'S SHOES 1	129
WALKING IN ANOTHER PERSON'S SHOES 2	132
MIRROR NEURONS	135
DIFFERENT POINTS OF VIEW	138

Empathy

Walking in another person's shoes 1

SESSION OBJECTIVES

To look at a situation from another person's point of view.

SESSION OUTCOMES

✓ To be able to say how someone else may be feeling.

✓ To be able to describe what empathy is to a partner.

LESSON PLAN

➢ Remind the children about one of their class baby observations when they were able to understand how their baby was feeling.

➢ Discuss the word 'empathy' and what it means.

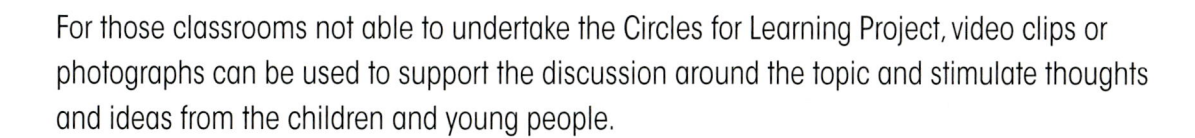

For those classrooms not able to undertake the Circles for Learning Project, video clips or photographs can be used to support the discussion around the topic and stimulate thoughts and ideas from the children and young people.

Task

KS1: To identify the feelings of another person.
KS2/3: To be able to describe what empathy is and to be able to describe how other people may be feeling and why.
To be able to make an empathy definition picture/word definition.

Empathy

KS1

1. Read the book *Stand in My Shoes* by Bob Sornson. Discuss what the book is trying to help us understand. How can we look at someone and understand how they feel?

2. Make the special empathy glasses with the children. When you wear these you can see more clearly how someone is feeling and why. Once the children have their glasses, put them into groups and share out the pictures. Ask each of the groups to put on their empathy glasses and look at the pictures.

3. Ask the children to draw how people are feeling in the thought bubbles and put them around the pictures.

4. Ask the children to discuss what the person might do next. This will allow them to understand that emotions do not last forever and soon pass.

5. Link this back to how the parent has to think about their class baby – the baby cannot talk and so a huge part of a parent's job is to attune to their baby and think about how they are feeling and why, and if they need to do something to make them feel better.

KS2/3

1. Share the video clip 'Stand in my shoes: Exposing and erasing the empathy deficit' with the children and discuss how the different people may be feeling and why.

2. Discuss the clues that the young people used.

    ➢ Facial expressions
    ➢ Body language
    ➢ Situation
    ➢ Other people around them

3. Link this to the role of a parent in understanding their class baby. Introduce the word 'attunement' and discuss its meaning.

4. Explore where we learn this skill.

5. Create an empathy definition poster either defining the word or making a picture to show the meaning.

6. Share these with each other.

RESOURCES

1. Large flip chart

2. Pens for flip chart

3. Sticky notes

Empathy

4. Paper and pens

5. Coloured pens

6. 'Stand in my shoes: Exposing and erasing the empathy deficit', http://www.kickstarter.com/projects/peacelily/stand-in-my-shoes-exposing-and-erasing-the-empathy (accessed 6 November 2018)

7. A selection of pictures showing people feeling a variety of different feelings.

8. *Stand in My Shoes* by Bob Sornson

IMPORTANT POINTS

- To explore how another person might feel.
- By thinking about other people we might want to change our behaviour.

LEARNING LINKS

Speaking and listening, collaboration, information processing, questioning, observation, creativity, planning and organisation, teamwork.

REFLECTION

Questions:

Positive comment from child:

Positive comment from adult:

LEARNING DIMENSIONS		SOCIAL & EMOTIONAL SKILLS	
Strategic awareness	🟧	Emotional literacy	🟩
Learning relationships		Neuroscience	
Curiosity	🟧	Self-regulation	
Creativity	🟧	Self-development	🟩
Meaning making	🟧		
Changing & learning	🟧		
Resilience	🟩		

Empathy

Walking in another person's shoes 2

SESSION OBJECTIVES

To look at a situation from another person's point of view.

SESSION OUTCOMES

✓ To work in groups to discuss and then put thoughts and feelings on to empathy pictures.

LESSON PLAN

➢ To help the children remember a time when the parent of their class baby had shown that they knew how their baby was feeling.

➢ To help the children remember a time when they had understood how their class baby felt and what enabled them to do this.

For those classrooms not able to undertake the Circles for Learning Project, video clips or photographs can be used to support the discussion around the topic and stimulate thoughts and ideas from the children and young people.

Task

KS1: To be able to share a range of pictures and describe how different people may be feeling and why.
KS2/3: To be able to share a range of pictures and say how people may be feeling and why.
To be able to explore different points of view.

KS1

1. Share a range of pictures with the children and discuss how people are feeling.

2. Help the children identify the evidence they are using to make these decisions.

Empathy

3. Choose one picture and then as a class show the different feelings of the people in the picture. Sticky notes or speech bubbles can be used to show how people are feeling.

4. Share the book *Stick and Stone* by Beth Ferry and Tom Lichtenheld.

5. Discuss how the different characters feel in the story.

KS2/3

1. Divide the class into groups of 4 and give each group a picture.

2. Ask them to think about each person in the picture and decide how they may be feeling – ask them to share their evidence for this.

3. Ask them to then say what they would do if they were a bystander – respond to another person's needs.

4. Link this with what a parent has to do with their class baby.

5. Discuss what it could feel like for a baby who has experienced a parent who seems to think about them and understand them or be attuned to them and what it must be like for a baby who has not experienced this.

RESOURCES

1. Large flip chart

2. Pens for flip chart

3. Sticky notes

4. Paper and pens

5. Coloured pens

6. Empathy pictures set – these need to show a group of people dealing with a situation where different people are experiencing different thoughts and feelings.

7. *Stick and Stone* by Beth Ferry and Tom Litchenheld

IMPORTANT POINTS

- To explore how another person might feel.

- By thinking about other people we might want to change our behaviour.

Empathy

LEARNING LINKS

Speaking and listening, collaboration, information processing, questioning, observation, creativity, planning and organisation, teamwork.

REFLECTION

Questions:

Positive comment from child:

Positive comment from adult:

LEARNING DIMENSIONS		SOCIAL & EMOTIONAL SKILLS	
Strategic awareness	🟧	Emotional literacy	🟩
Learning relationships		Neuroscience	
Curiosity	🟧	Self-regulation	
Creativity	🟧	Self-development	🟩
Meaning making	🟧		
Changing & learning	🟧		
Resilience	🟩		

Empathy

Mirror neurons

SESSION OBJECTIVES

To investigate how we learn to empathise with others, understand how they are feeling.

SESSION OUTCOMES

✓ To create a series of pictures to show how mirror neurons were discovered.

✓ To create a picture that causes the viewer to experience an emotion.

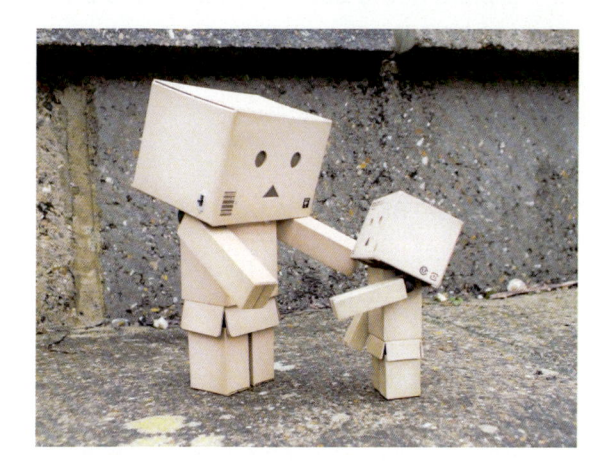

LESSON PLAN

➢ Remind the children about a time when they watched the parent interpret what their class baby wanted.

➢ Discuss empathy and attunement and revisit why it is such an important skill for a parent to develop.

For those classrooms not able to undertake the Circles for Learning Project, video clips or photographs can be used to support the discussion around the topic and stimulate thoughts and ideas from the children and young people.

Task

KS1: To be able to draw a picture that makes the audience feel something, i.e. happy, sad, frightened.

1. Share with the children the story of the monkey and how mirror neurons were discovered.

2. Ask them to draw a picture that will make the viewer feel an emotion.

3. Share the pictures in a silent exhibition. Ask the children to write down the feeling that they think each picture makes them experience.

KS2: To be able to describe or draw how mirror neurons were found and why they are important.

1. Share the 'RSA Animate: The empathic civilisation' video clip and discuss.

Empathy

2. Ask the young people to create their own series of pictures to describe what mirror neurons are.

3. Explore how a baby may feel with a parent who is attuned to their needs and how a baby may feel if a parent struggles to interpret their needs.

RESOURCES

1. Sticky notes
2. Paper and pens
3. Coloured pens
4. 'RSA ANIMATE: The empathic civilisation', https://www.youtube.com/watch?v=l7AWnfFRc7g
5. 'Mirror neurons part 1', https://www.youtube.com/watch?v=XzMqPYfeA-s
6. 'Mirror neurons, part 2', https://www.youtube.com/watch?v=xmEsGQ3JmKg

IMPORTANT POINTS

- To understand how mirror neurons support us in understanding another person and the benefits of this.
- Linking how our emotional response is triggered and why we behave as we do.

LEARNING LINKS

Speaking and listening, collaboration, information processing, questioning, observation, creativity, planning and organisation, teamwork.

REFLECTION

Questions:

Positive comment from child:

Positive comment from adult:

Empathy

LEARNING DIMENSIONS		SOCIAL & EMOTIONAL SKILLS	
Strategic awareness	🟧	Emotional literacy	🟩
Learning relationships		Neuroscience	
Curiosity	🟧	Self-regulation	
Creativity	🟧	Self-development	🟩
Meaning making	🟧		
Changing & learning	🟧		
Resilience	🟩		

Empathy

Different points of view

SESSION OBJECTIVES

To investigate how empathy allows us to be more flexible in our responses and behaviour towards others.

SESSION OUTCOMES

- ✓ To be able to act out a short play and explore the different feelings of the characters.

LESSON PLAN

- ➢ Recap on the word 'empathy' and what it means.

- ➢ Recap on how mirror neurons work and how they allow us to feel what another person is experiencing.

For those classrooms not able to undertake the Circles for Learning Project, video clips or photographs can be used to support the discussion around the topic and stimulate thoughts and ideas from the children and young people.

Task

KS2/KS3: To explore empathy through role play.

1. Discuss how acting requires the actor to understand how a character may be feeling and why and then share that with the audience.

2. Set the groups up and ask them to act out the Neighbourhood Nightmare.

3. On the role card, write what each person is feeling and why.

4. After 3 minutes they need to change role.

Empathy

5. Each young person needs to experience 2 different roles.

6. Write on role cards the response they need to enable them to feel more positive/better and why.

7. Discuss how the acting made them feel.

8. What other things did this bring up for them?

9. Link how we feel to how we behave and how we feel to how we want someone to respond.

RESOURCES

1. Blanket
2. Role play scenarios
3. Role play character cards
4. Pens and paper

IMPORTANT POINTS

- To understand how mirror neurons support us in understanding another person and the benefits of this in making our responses more flexible.

- Linking our emotional response to others and our behaviour.

LEARNING LINKS

Speaking and listening, collaboration, information processing, questioning, observation, creativity, planning and organisation, teamwork.

REFLECTION

Questions:

Positive comment from child:

Positive comment from adult:

Empathy

LEARNING DIMENSIONS		SOCIAL & EMOTIONAL SKILLS	
Strategic awareness	🟧	Emotional literacy	🟩
Learning relationships		Neuroscience	
Curiosity	🟧	Self-regulation	
Creativity	🟧	Self-development	🟩
Meaning making	🟧		
Changing & learning	🟧		
Resilience	🟩		

Empathy

ROLE PLAY SCENARIOS

The local school keeps getting broken into and vandalised.

Caretaker – Mr Smith is very fed up as he is having to clear everything up and he isn't able to get on with the jobs he needs to.

Older lady who lives opposite the school. Mrs Silver is in her 80s and lives alone now her husband has died. She is frightened by the noises she hears at night and from the stories she reads about in the local paper.

Teenagers – Colin, Tam, Pete and Nim all live near the school and like to meet up outside the corner shop and have a laugh. People keep treating them as if it is them that keep vandalising the school.

Ted and Chaz are two teenagers who have been excluded from the school as the school is not able to meet their needs and they have been violent towards other children and staff. They are angry with the school and have been breaking in to wind people up.

Mr and Mrs Stevens own the corner shop and get on well with the teenagers as their son often hangs out with them.

Mrs Frant is the Head Teacher of the school. She is cross that the school keeps getting broken into and vandalised. She and her staff have worked hard to create a good environment for the children and the vandalisation is costing the school money that they want to spend on other things.

PC Becker is the local policeman who is trying to make sure that the school is kept safe and who wants to catch the people who are causing so much trouble to the area.

A group of young people keep shoplifting in the local corner shop.

Mrs George works in the shop and keeps being blamed by the owners for not catching who is stealing from them.

Mr and Mrs Shilling own the shop and have worked hard to get it well established and making money as they are supporting their two daughters who are at University. They are thinking of closing the shop.

Bob, Shane and Raj plus a few other teenagers are all part of a group that dares each other to steal from the shop. They think it is funny.

Dan, Mark and Digby all go to the shop on their way home from school. They don't like the fact that they are always being watched and feel like people think they are the thieves. They have now stopped going to the shop but have found another one down the road.

Ted Oliver is an elderly gentleman in his 90s. He has been visiting the corner shop here since he was a young boy and uses it every day as a way of talking and meeting people. Since his wife died he gets very lonely.

Mrs Webster is the owner of 'Shop Video', a business that sells and then maintains shop video cameras. She has just been asked to install 4 cameras in the corner shop.

Empathy

ROLE PLAY CHARACTER CARDS	
Mr Smith Caretaker	**Mrs Silver** Neighbour to school
Colin/Tam/Pete/Nim Teenagers who live close to school	**Ted/Chaz** Teenagers who have been excluded from school
Mr and Mrs Stevens Shop owner and parents of a teenager at the school	**Mrs Frant** Head Teacher
PC Becker Local policeman	
Mrs George Works in the local corner shop	**Mr and Mrs Shilling** Own the local corner shop
Bob/Shane/Raj Teenagers who dare each other to shoplift	**Dan/Mark/Digby** Teenagers who visit the shop each day
Ted Oliver Elderly man who uses the shop	**Mrs Webster** 'Shop Video' owner

Chapter 7
Self-efficacy and responsibility

SELF-ESTEEM: WHAT WE BELIEVE ABOUT OURSELVES	145
ONLY ONE OF YOU	151
SELF-ESTEEM, SELF-LIMITING BELIEFS	155
MY 'I DID IT' GALLERY	162
PEOPLE WE ADMIRE	166
GET TO KNOW YOUR BEST FRIEND	170
YOU ARE YOUR OWN BEST FRIEND	174
BE YOUR OWN LIFE COACH	180

Self-efficacy and responsibility

Self-esteem: What we believe about ourselves

SESSION OBJECTIVES

To develop a greater understanding of how we decide what to believe about ourselves.

SESSION OUTCOMES

✓ A range of labels that we have collected about ourselves.

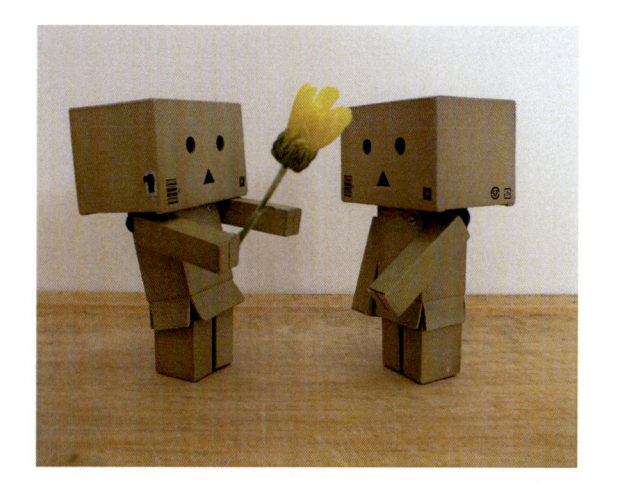

LESSON PLAN

➢ Ask the children and young people to remember a time when the parent has given a label to their class baby: 'She is so good at sleeping' 'He is such a fuss pot'.

➢ Ask the children to think of labels that they have been given. Give examples of ones that you carry.

For those classrooms not able to undertake the Circles for Learning Project, video clips or photographs can be used to support the discussion around the topic and stimulate thoughts and ideas from the children and young people.

Task

KS1: Draw a picture of themselves with 6 labels they have been given.
　　 Write three labels they would like to be given in the future.
KS2: To be able to list the labels that Maisy is given in the story.
　　 To be able to write six labels that they have been given.
　　 To create four labels they would like to achieve over the year ahead.

KS1

1. Remind the children of the labels that their class baby is collecting all the time.

2. Ask them to think of labels that they have been given. Write them on sticky notes. Choose yellow for ones they like and pink for ones they don't like.

Self-efficacy and responsibility

3. Ask them to draw a picture of themselves and stick the labels around the picture.

4. Ask the children to write 3 labels they would like to collect in the future.

5. Share with each other what they need to do to collect them. Add these to their picture.

KS2

1. Share the story 'Maisy's Day' with the young people.

2. In pairs ask them to write on a sticky note all the labels she is given that day.

3. Divide the pile up into positive ones and negative ones.

4. Ask the young people to share a label that they have been given and let them explore what they think about it.

5. Demonstrate with Maisy's picture that the labels can be taken off if she doesn't want them.

6. Ask the young people to come up with 4 labels they would like to collect over the year ahead.

7. In pairs, discuss what they could do or how they might work to achieve them.

RESOURCES

1. Large flip chart
2. Pens for flip chart
3. Sticky notes
4. Paper and pens
5. Coloured pens
6. Labels sheet
7. Sticky labels/luggage tags

IMPORTANT POINTS

- We have a choice over whether we take a label and how we behave.

Self-efficacy and responsibility

LEARNING LINKS

Speaking and listening, collaboration, information processing, questioning, observation, creativity, planning and organisation, teamwork.

REFLECTION

Questions:

Positive comment from child:

Positive comment from adult:

LEARNING DIMENSIONS		SOCIAL & EMOTIONAL SKILLS	
Strategic awareness	🟧	Emotional literacy	🟩
Learning relationships		Neuroscience	
Curiosity	🟧	Self-regulation	
Creativity	🟧	Self-development	🟩
Meaning making	🟧		
Changing & learning	🟧		
Resilience	🟩		

Self-efficacy and responsibility

MAISY'S DAY

The alarm went off and Maisy leapt out of bed. She needed to get a shower and wash her hair as she was going to audition for the school play. She got her things ready but her big sister was in the shower. She yelled for her to hurry up, telling her she needed to shower. Her Mum called up the stairs telling her to be quiet. 'You are always so loud Maisy; leave your sister to shower.'

Maisy tried to explain to her Mum why it was so important.

'If it was that important then you should have told your sister last night, really you are so disorganised.'

Maisy gathered up all her stuff but couldn't find her school bag. She called down to her Mum to see if she had seen it but Mum just told her to look for it where she had last left it!! 'Honestly Maisy, you really are forgetful.'

Finally her sister was out of the shower – quickly Maisy dashed in and slammed the door. She frantically got showered and washed her hair and then dashed back to her bedroom to dry it. Mum came into her bedroom and threw her towel at her. 'Maisy you are so untidy, please clean up after yourself. I'm fed up with doing it.'

Maisy quickly hung up her towel and then dashed downstairs for breakfast. Her little brother was struggling with the milk container lid. Maisy gave him a tickle and then helped him. He giggled and smiled at her. 'I love you Maisy,' he said as he gave her a cuddle. Mum looked up and smiled at Maisy.

'You know you really are good with your brother. Thank you.'

Maisy then grabbed all her things and dashed to the car. Her Dad was waiting to take her to school. She leapt in and then slammed the door. Dad frowned. He was not happy.

'Maisy I wish you would treat things with more respect. You really seem to have no idea about how to look after things.'

Maisy apologised and then sorted out her homework. Dad smiled. 'You know, when your Mum and I went to parents evening your Maths teacher was really pleased with your progress. He said you had been really working hard and that you were really focused in his class. Shame the Science teacher didn't think so, he said you often forgot your homework and were always talking to your friends. He said you were a really disruptive student. I can't understand how you can be so different.'

'I know Dad. I just really like the maths teacher, he really helps me.'

Maisy and her Dad finally got to school. 'Is it the auditions day today?' asked Dad.

Self-efficacy and responsibility

'Yes,' said Maisy.

'I hope it goes well, you deserve it. You have worked really hard on learning your lines, you really do have a great memory and I know I am your Dad but I also think you have a lot of talent.'

'Thanks Dad, fingers crossed.'

Maisy jumped out of the car and went into school. As she walked in through the doors, her friends came to meet her and they all walked to their form room together. As they entered, Mr Smith the Deputy Head came in. He handed out the timetables for the auditions, Maisy was so excited to get one that she forgot to say thank you when he handed her the sheet.

'You know Maisy Turner, you really are one of the rudest students I know, not only don't you say please and thank you but I also saw you teasing one of the Year 7s the other day. I've got my eye on you so I suggest that you sort yourself out.'

'Yes Sir,' answered Maisy.

'What was all that about?' asked her friend.

'I'm not sure. He seems to have it in for me, he's rather full of himself.'

Maisy grabbed the timetable and then set off for Maths, which was her first lesson. Mr Brown met her at the door. 'How's my grade A student doing? Did you manage the homework?'

Maisy nodded and smiled 'Yes Sir, I did, once I got going it was fine.'

'Well done Maisy. I really do think you have a brain for maths, you will go far.'

'Thanks Sir.'

Maisy finished Maths and then went off for the audition. She was really nervous and didn't see Mr Smith walk around the corner. She bumped into him and knocked his books flying. 'Oh God I am really sorry Sir, I wasn't concentrating I was trying to . . .'

'I don't want to hear your excuses young lady. You need to look where you're going. I am putting you in a lunchtime detention for running in the corridors. Perhaps that way you will learn that you are not the only person in this school.'

Maisy went to argue but then drew a deep breath and remembered the audition. Instead she smiled and said 'Yes Sir,' before turning and escaping into the drama room.

Self-efficacy and responsibility

Self-efficacy and responsibility

Only one of you

SESSION OBJECTIVES

To enable children to explore the uniqueness of themselves.

To enable children to celebrate who they are.

SESSION OUTCOMES

✓ To identify a range of qualities and characteristics that make them unique.

✓ To be able to create an advice phrase for themselves that will support them over the year ahead.

LESSON PLAN

➢ Ask the children to think about their class baby and identify a time when they were aware of a comment made by their parent that started to identify something special or unique about them.

➢ Ask the children to discuss how these comments/behaviours might influence the child in the future.

For those classrooms not able to undertake the Circles for Learning Project, video clips or photographs can be used to support the discussion around the topic and stimulate thoughts and ideas from the children and young people.

Task

KS1: To create a fish that is unique.
KS2/3: To create an advice saying to support themselves during the year ahead.

KS1/2

1. Read the book *Only One You* by Linda Kranz.

2. Ask the children why they think that the parents wanted to share advice with their young fish.

3. Talk about the other fish in the pictures – are they different? Does each fish need the same advice? What makes people different?

Self-efficacy and responsibility

4. Ask the children to

   KS1. Make a fish and decorate it. This could be a pebble fish or a paper fish with collage scales.
   KS2. Make a saying in a medium of their choice for themselves to support them over the year ahead. This could be drawn, made from card, modelling clay, collage work or fabric.

5. The work can then be displayed showing the individuals and their advice phrases for the year ahead.

KS3

1. After discussing the baby observations and the parent's interpretation of their baby's behaviour or attributes, ask the children, 'What makes us all different?'

2. Record their ideas.

   Include – different experiences, different characteristics, different skills, abilities, likes and dislikes. Support the children in thinking about why they might enjoy things, for example cooking, which was was something that they did with their grandmother and they very much enjoyed. Or skateboarding – they enjoyed the thrill and challenging themselves to get better.

3. Show a picture of pebbles – each pebble is unique and different.

4. Ask the children to think of an advice phrase that they feel is important. It might be 'to live life to the full', 'YOLO – You only live once', 'Keep going', 'When the going gets tough dig in', etc. Research on the internet for the different sayings. Explore different tattoos as many have positive sayings.

5. Ask the young people to design and create an advice phrase using a range of ways – clay, pastels, painting photographs etc. This could also be a tattoo.

6. Ask the children to share the sayings and why they think they are important.

RESOURCES

1. Sticky notes

2. Plain paper and pens

3. Pebble picture

4. Tattoos

Self-efficacy and responsibility

IMPORTANT POINTS

Sayings can help us manage and keep going.

We are unique individuals and that is what makes us special.

LEARNING LINKS

Speaking and listening, collaboration, information processing, questioning, observation, creativity, planning and organisation, teamwork.

REFLECTION

Questions:

Positive comment from child:

Positive comment from adult:

LEARNING DIMENSIONS		SOCIAL & EMOTIONAL SKILLS	
Strategic awareness	🟧	Emotional literacy	🟩
Learning relationships		Neuroscience	
Curiosity	🟧	Self-regulation	
Creativity	🟧	Self-development	🟩
Meaning making	🟧		
Changing & learning	🟧		
Resilience	🟩		

Self-efficacy and responsibility

Self-efficacy and responsibility

Self-esteem, self-limiting beliefs

SESSION OBJECTIVES

To develop a greater understanding about how our beliefs about ourselves impact on what we do and what we think we can do.

SESSION OUTCOMES

✓ To be able to share the story of the elephant.

✓ To create a beliefs systems triangle poster.

LESSON PLAN

➢ Ask the children to remember when they had observed the parent give their class baby a label.

➢ Remind the children and young people about the work on labels.

For those classrooms not able to undertake the Circles for Learning Project, video clips or photographs can be used to support the discussion around the topic and stimulate thoughts and ideas from the children and young people.

Task

KS1: Be able to retell the elephant story and explain how our beliefs can limit what we do or allow us to do great things.
KS2: To create a beliefs systems triangle poster.

KS1
1. Remind the children about their work on labels.

2. Read them the story about the elephant.

3. Discuss what the story helps us to understand about ourselves and what we believe.

4. Draw a picture to illustrate the elephant story.

Copyright material from Alison Waterhouse (2019), *Self-Discovery*, Routledge

Self-efficacy and responsibility

KS2

1. Discuss the work already done on labels and how they impact on how we think about ourselves.

2. Discuss our beliefs or self-esteem and how it can change depending on what we are doing. If we think we are good at maths then we probably will be. If we have maths in the morning then our self-esteem will be high. If we don't think we are very good at art and we have art in the afternoon then our self-esteem will be lower.

3. Share the beliefs systems triangle poster.

4. Discuss.

5. Put up the 'A mind stretched to a new idea never returns to its original dimension' quote.

6. Ask the young people to make a poster to show the belief systems triangle.

7. Agree the success criteria. These may include:

   Must show the link between beliefs, experiences and behaviour
   That we have a choice about how we think about things
   It must be eye catching so that people stop and look
   It must be easy to read
   It must get the message across that we have choices about what we believe about ourselves.

8. Display all the posters – small versions could be made to go in the front of books or to make a patchwork display.

RESOURCES

1. Paper and pens

2. Elephant story

3. Beliefs systems triangle

4. Mind-stretcher quote

IMPORTANT POINTS

- What we believe about ourselves influences how we behave and what we do.

- We have a choice as to whether we challenge our beliefs and behave in a different way.

Self-efficacy and responsibility

LEARNING LINKS

Speaking and listening, collaboration, information processing, questioning, observation, creativity, planning and organisation, teamwork.

REFLECTION

Questions:

Positive comment from child:

Positive comment from adult:

LEARNING DIMENSIONS		SOCIAL & EMOTIONAL SKILLS	
Strategic awareness	🟧	Emotional literacy	🟩
Learning relationships		Neuroscience	
Curiosity	🟧	Self-regulation	
Creativity	🟧	Self-development	🟩
Meaning making	🟧		
Changing & learning	🟧		
Resilience	🟩		

Self-efficacy and responsibility

A mind stretched to a new idea never returns to its original dimension.

Self-efficacy and responsibility

Copyright material from Alison Waterhouse (2019), *Self-Discovery*, Routledge

159

Self-efficacy and responsibility

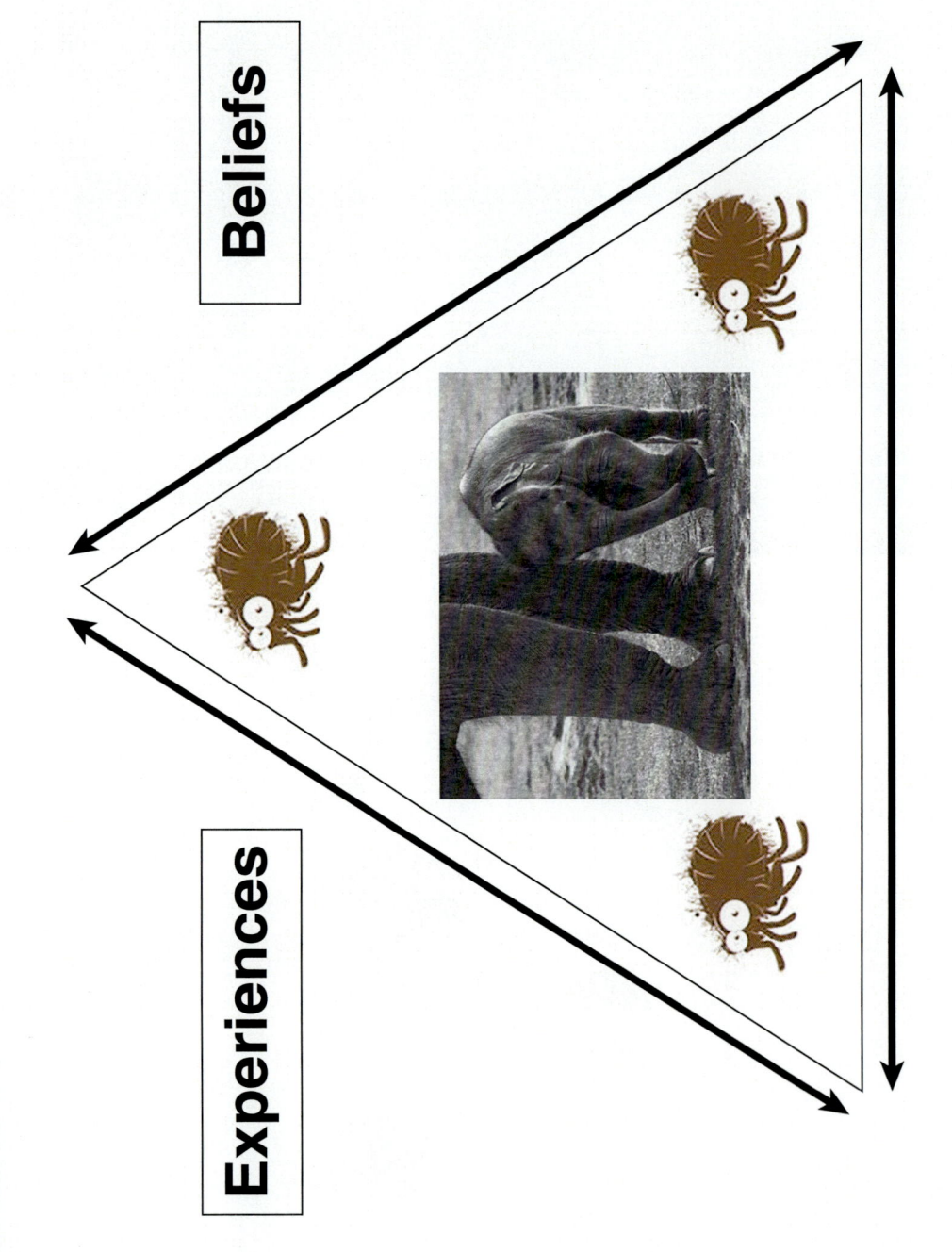

THE BELIEFS SYSTEMS TRIANGLE

Beliefs

Choices

Experiences

THE ELEPHANT

What we believe about ourselves and the world actually creates the world we live in even if the belief is totally false.

Did you know that you can take a two tonne elephant, put a thin rope around its ankle and attach it to a small wooden peg in the ground and the elephant will not move?

The elephant could of course pull the stake out of the ground in an instant and go off whereever it wanted to and have a wonderful time. So why doesn't it?

When it was a baby elephant, a heavy chain was attached to its ankle and it was tied to a strong post in the ground. It learnt that every time it tried to get away it couldn't and if it kept trying it hurt its ankle. Consequently it grew up with the belief 'If you put a tie around my ankle then I cannot move.' A totally false belief in this instance. In fact elephants have been known to die in fires tethered in this fashion because they believed they could not move.

Fleas have been shown to do a similar thing. A flea can jump 18 cm upwards from the table which, given the fact that it is only 2.5mm long, is quite amazing. It would be the same as us jumping over a 30 storey building. However, if a flea grows up in a jar it learns to only jump the height of the jar – or it hits its head. If you then take the lid off the jar the flea will still only jump to the height it has learnt is safe – which means it doesn't escape.

This is exactly what your BELIEFS are like – both the good ones and the not so helpful ones. They are like a rope around your ankle keeping you from doing things in your life.

Self-efficacy and responsibility

My 'I did it' gallery

SESSION OBJECTIVES

To enable children to identify when they achieved something difficult.

To enable children to identify the strategies that they used to achieve something difficult.

SESSION OUTCOMES

✓ To celebrate achievements and understand how resilience grows over time.

LESSON PLAN

➢ Ask the children to think about their class baby and identify a time when they persevered and achieved something difficult.

➢ Ask the children what they think enabled the baby to do this.

➢ List the ideas/strategies they used or that the parent used to support the baby.

For those classrooms not able to undertake the Circles for Learning Project, video clips or photographs can be used to support the discussion around the topic and stimulate thoughts and ideas from the children and young people.

Task

KS1: To create a gallery of achievements.
   To identify the strategies they used to do something difficult and to explore how their resilience has developed and grown as they have experienced learning and life.
KS2/3: To create a gallery of achievements and celebrate what they are able to do.
   To identify strategies that support them and those that undermine them developing resilience.

Note

The more they have been able to achieve, the more positively they think about their own capabilities. If a parent does everything for a child, then the child never learns to do things and

Self-efficacy and responsibility

the belief the parent inadvertently gives is 'you need me, you are not able'. An adult can steal the learning. If however we struggle too much then we give up and this reinforces a belief that we are no good.

As teachers we have to adapt work so that it is stretching.

KS1
1. Ask the children to work in pairs and discuss what they could put into the gallery sheet, identifying things they have achieved that were stretching and difficult. Ask them to list the strategies that supported them achieving their goal or that kept them going.

2. Share with the class the things they have achieved at the different ages.

KS2/3
3. Using the children and young people's gallery to create a positive strategies list and a negative strategies list.

4. Link the positive ways of thinking and encouragement they have experienced to how they can treat themselves – develop self-talk.

RESOURCES

1. Sticky notes
2. Plain paper and pens
3. Gallery sheet
4. Red and green marker pens
5. Ladder picture

IMPORTANT POINTS

If we believe we can do something then we will keep trying.

If we have experienced success then we believe we can achieve.

If you think you can, you will. If you think you can't, you won't!!

LEARNING LINKS

Speaking and listening, collaboration, information processing, questioning, observation, creativity, planning and organisation, teamwork.

Self-efficacy and responsibility

REFLECTION

Questions:

Positive comment from child:

Positive comment from adult:

LEARNING DIMENSIONS		SOCIAL & EMOTIONAL SKILLS	
Strategic awareness	🟧	Emotional literacy	🟩
Learning relationships		Neuroscience	
Curiosity	🟧	Self-regulation	
Creativity	🟧	Self-development	🟩
Meaning making	🟧		
Changing & learning	🟧		
Resilience	🟩		

Self-efficacy and responsibility

Self-efficacy and responsibility

People we admire

SESSION OBJECTIVES

To identify people we admire.

To identify the skills, characteristics and qualities of these people.

SESSION OUTCOMES

- ✓ To identify a person we admire and identify the skills, characteristics and qualities that they have that we respect and appreciate.

- ✓ To identify qualities and characteristics in ourselves that we wish to develop and extend.

LESSON PLAN

➢ Ask the children to think about their class baby. What are the qualities that the baby has that they really admire/like?

➢ Ask the children to think about the baby's parent. What are the qualities that they display that they admire/like?

For those classrooms not able to undertake the Circles for Learning Project, video clips or photographs can be used to support the discussion around the topic and stimulate thoughts and ideas from the children and young people.

Task

KS1: To identify qualities, skills or characteristics that they admire.
    To identify 3 qualities that they are proud of in themselves.

KS2/3: To identify qualities skills or characteristics that they admire.
    To identify 3 qualities, 3 skills and 3 characteristics that they are proud of in themselves.
    To identify one characteristic that they would like to develop in themselves.

Self-efficacy and responsibility

1. Choose a book or story and ask the children to think of the main character (*Harry Potter* is good for KS3, *The Tin Forest* by Helen Ward and Wayne Anderson for KS2, 'Goldilocks and the Three Bears'/'Little Red Riding Hood' for KS1).

2. Identify the aspects of that character that they like and admire. Make a class list of skills, characteristics and qualities. Everyone has a unique profile and is good at a range of things. We are all different.

3. Choose a famous person and discuss a character profile, sharing what they like and admire.

4. Ask the children to draw a picture of themselves and then put one skill in or by each arm and leg, three qualities in or by their head and three characteristics in or by their middle.

5. Discuss with a partner one skill and characteristic that they wish to develop over the next term. Discuss the ways they could do this.

6. Ask them to write one skill and characteristic that they wish to develop over the next term on their sheet.

RESOURCES

1. Sticky notes
2. Person template
3. Plain paper and pens
4. Books: *The Tin Forest*, *Harry Potter*, 'Goldilocks and the Three Bears', 'Little Red Riding Hood'
5. Definitions of a skill, characteristic and a quality
6. Pictures of famous people – Barack Obama, Nelson Mandela, Thomas Edison, Martin Luther King, Mahatma Gandhi, Mother Teresa, with brief descriptions of them

IMPORTANT POINTS

We can choose who we are and how we would like to be.

Identifying the skills that we have and the ones that we would like to foster.

LEARNING LINKS

Speaking and listening, collaboration, information processing, questioning, observation, creativity, planning and organisation, teamwork.

Self-efficacy and responsibility

REFLECTION

Questions:

Positive comment from child:

Positive comment from adult:

LEARNING DIMENSIONS		SOCIAL & EMOTIONAL SKILLS	
Strategic awareness	🟧	Emotional literacy	🟩
Learning relationships		Neuroscience	
Curiosity	🟧	Self-regulation	
Creativity	🟧	Self-development	🟩
Meaning making	🟧		
Changing & learning	🟧		
Resilience	🟩		

Skill: The ability to do something well

Quality: A distinctive attribute or characteristic possessed by someone or something

Characteristic: A feature or quality of a person

Self-efficacy and responsibility

Get to know your best friend

SESSION OBJECTIVES

To explore the Thoughts, Feelings, Actions Triangle.

SESSION OUTCOMES

- ✓ Understand the Thoughts, Feelings, Actions Triangle and the impact it can have.

- ✓ A Friendship Wheel with positive comments about their best friend – themself!

LESSON PLAN

➢ Ask the children to think about their class baby and their interactions with their parent. How does the parent look at the baby?

➢ What does the baby experience when they get this 'look of love'?

For those classrooms not able to undertake the Circles for Learning Project, video clips or photographs can be used to support the discussion around the topic and stimulate thoughts and ideas from the children and young people.

Task

KS1: To write a positive comment to say to their best friend every day.
KS2: To complete the Friendship Wheel about themselves as their own best friend.
   To write a range of positive things to say to their best friend.

KS1

1. Give each child an envelope with the statement 'This is your best friend'.

2. Ask them to open up the envelope and see if you have got it right for all the class. Inside each envelope put a mirror so they see themselves as they open the envelope.

Self-efficacy and responsibility

3. Remind the children about the Thoughts, Feelings, Actions Triangle and that what we think about ourselves links to what we do and how we feel.

4. Ask the children to write a positive note to themselves to read every day.

KS2

1. Give each child an envelope with the statement 'This is your best friend'.

2. Ask them to open up the envelope and see if you have got it right for all the class. Inside each envelope put a mirror so they see themselves as they open the envelope.

3. Remind the children about the Thoughts, Feelings, Actions Triangle and that what we think about ourselves links to what we do and how we feel.

4. Give the children the Friendship Wheel and ask them to fill it in about themselves.

5. Pair up the children so that they can share their wheels.

6. Ask the partners to add something to the wheel – remind the young people that it needs to be positive.

7. Ask the young people to write a positive note to themselves.

RESOURCES

1. Sticky notes

2. Friendship Wheel

3. Mirrors – enough for one each and placed inside an envelope

4. Thoughts, Feelings, Actions Triangle

5. Postcards/speech bubble sticky notes

IMPORTANT POINTS

If we do not like or love ourselves, how can we expect anyone else to.

LEARNING LINKS

Speaking and listening, collaboration, information processing, questioning, observation, creativity, planning and organisation, teamwork.

Self-efficacy and responsibility

REFLECTION

Questions:

Positive comment from child:

Positive comment from adult:

LEARNING DIMENSIONS		SOCIAL & EMOTIONAL SKILLS	
Strategic awareness	🟧	Emotional literacy	🟩
Learning relationships		Neuroscience	
Curiosity	🟧	Self-regulation	
Creativity	🟧	Self-development	🟩
Meaning making	🟧		
Changing & learning	🟧		
Resilience	🟩		

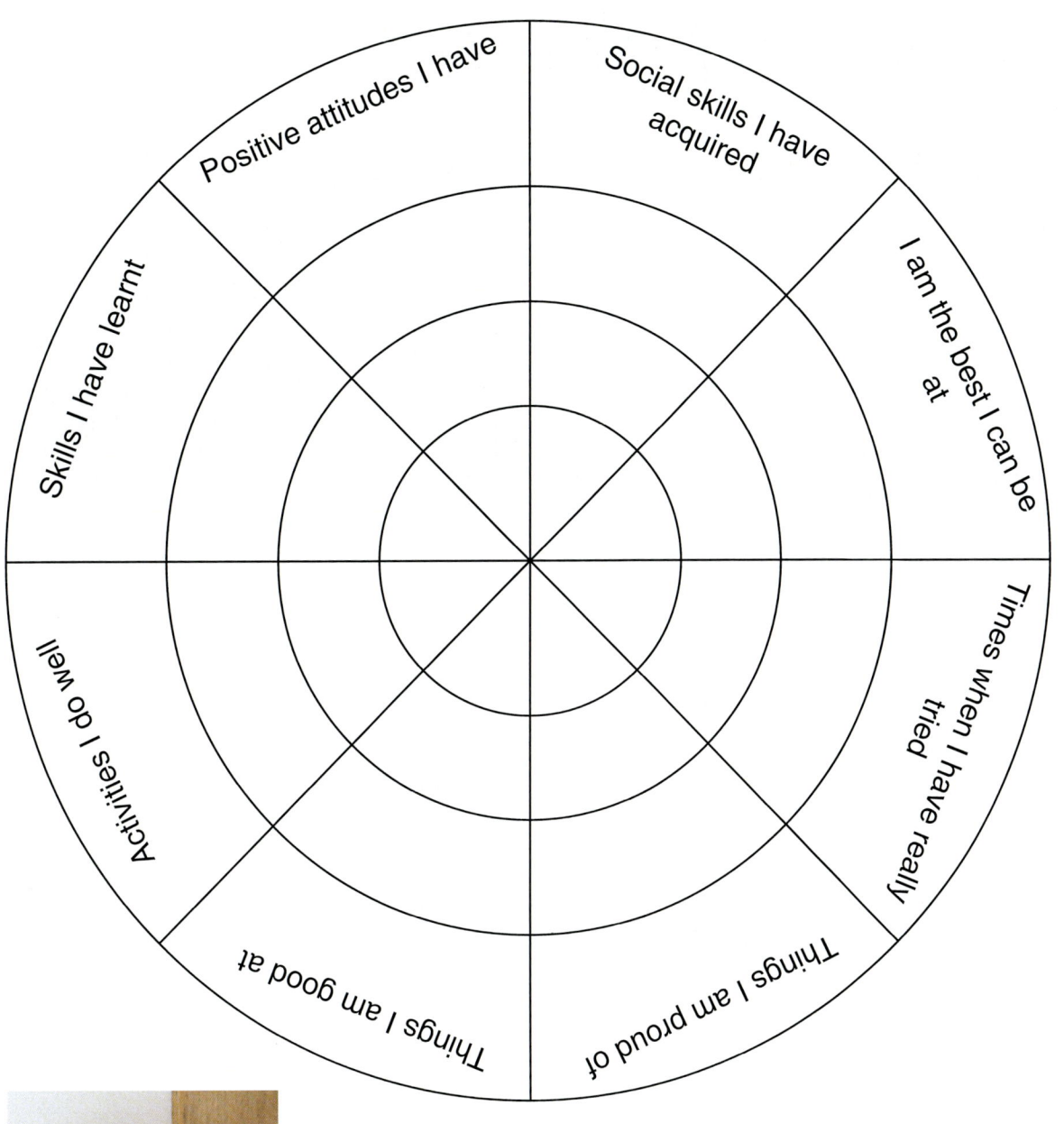

Self-efficacy and responsibility

Friendship Wheel

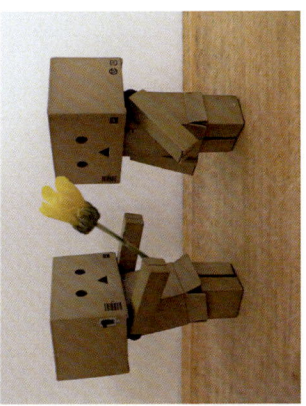

Segments of the wheel (clockwise from top):
- Social skills I have acquired
- I am the best I can be at
- Times when I have really tried
- Things I am proud of
- Things I am good at
- Activities I do well
- Skills I have learnt
- Positive attitudes I have

Copyright material from Alison Waterhouse (2019), *Self-Discovery*, Routledge

173

Self-efficacy and responsibility

You are your own best friend

SESSION OBJECTIVES

To identify skills and qualities that make a best friend.

To explore how you can become your own best friend.

SESSION OUTCOMES

- ✓ To create a best friend bookmark. KS1
- ✓ To create a best friend quote book. KS2/KS3

LESSON PLAN

- ➢ Share a clip or remind the children of a time when their class baby turned to their parent. Explore what they wanted and what the parent did. Did they need reassurance, support, calming or helping in some way.

- ➢ Ask 'What happens if Mum or Dad are not accessible when you need them?'

- ➢ Explore with the children ways that they deal with this.

For those classrooms not able to undertake the Circles for Learning Project, video clips or photographs can be used to support the discussion around the topic and stimulate thoughts and ideas from the children and young people.

Task

KS1: To identify qualities, skills or characteristics of a best friend.
    To create a best friend bookmark.
KS2/3: To identify qualities skills or characteristics of a best friend.
    To create a best friend quote book.
    To identify 3 ways that they could become a better best friend to themselves.

Self-efficacy and responsibility

KS1/2

1. Choose a book or story and ask the children to think of the main character. Ask them to identify ways in which the character is or could be their own best friend.

   KS1 – 'Jack and the Beanstalk'
   KS2 – *The Most Magnificent Thing* by Ashley Spires

2. Share the ideas that they come up with and create a list of examples.

3. Help the children create positive phrases that the character could say.

   'I can do this'
   'I can problem solve'
   'I am good at puzzles'
   'When I get home this will be such a good story'
   'Keep going'

4. Add them to the story as speech bubbles.

5. Create the bookmarks with the children drawing themselves or using photos of themselves. Fill in the speech bubbles they like the most and which they think will be the most helpful when they get stuck.

KS3

1. Ask the young people to think of a story or film where the main character is being supported by their friends – e.g. Harry Potter.

2. Ask them to identify their top ten friendships skills with a partner.

3. Ask the young people to design a character that represents themselves or use a photo or a drawing of their face and create a best friend quote book. On each page they need to put their character or photo/drawing and a speech bubble to show encouraging words a friend might say when the going gets tough.

4. Identify the friendship skill they think they could develop that would be supportive to them when the going gets tough, over the next term. Discuss the ways they could do this with their partner.

5. Have a silent exhibition to show off the work. Lay out the work on the tables and allow the young people to go and look at the different examples of the work.

Self-efficacy and responsibility

RESOURCES

1. Sticky notes
2. Bookmark template
3. Photos of the children
4. Plain paper and pens
5. Books: – 'Jack and the Beanstalk', *The Most Magnificent Thing* by Ashley Spires
6. Speech bubbles
7. Bookmark master
8. How to make a book

IMPORTANT POINTS

We are our own best friend.

Identifying the skills that we have and the ones that we would like to foster.

LEARNING LINKS

Speaking and listening, collaboration, information processing, questioning, observation, creativity, planning and organisation, teamwork.

REFLECTION

Questions:

Positive comment from child:

Positive comment from adult:

Self-efficacy and responsibility

LEARNING DIMENSIONS		SOCIAL & EMOTIONAL SKILLS	
Strategic awareness	🟧	Emotional literacy	🟩
Learning relationships		Neuroscience	
Curiosity	🟧	Self-regulation	
Creativity	🟧	Self-development	🟩
Meaning making	🟧		
Changing & learning	🟧		
Resilience	🟩		

Self-efficacy and responsibility

Self-efficacy and responsibility

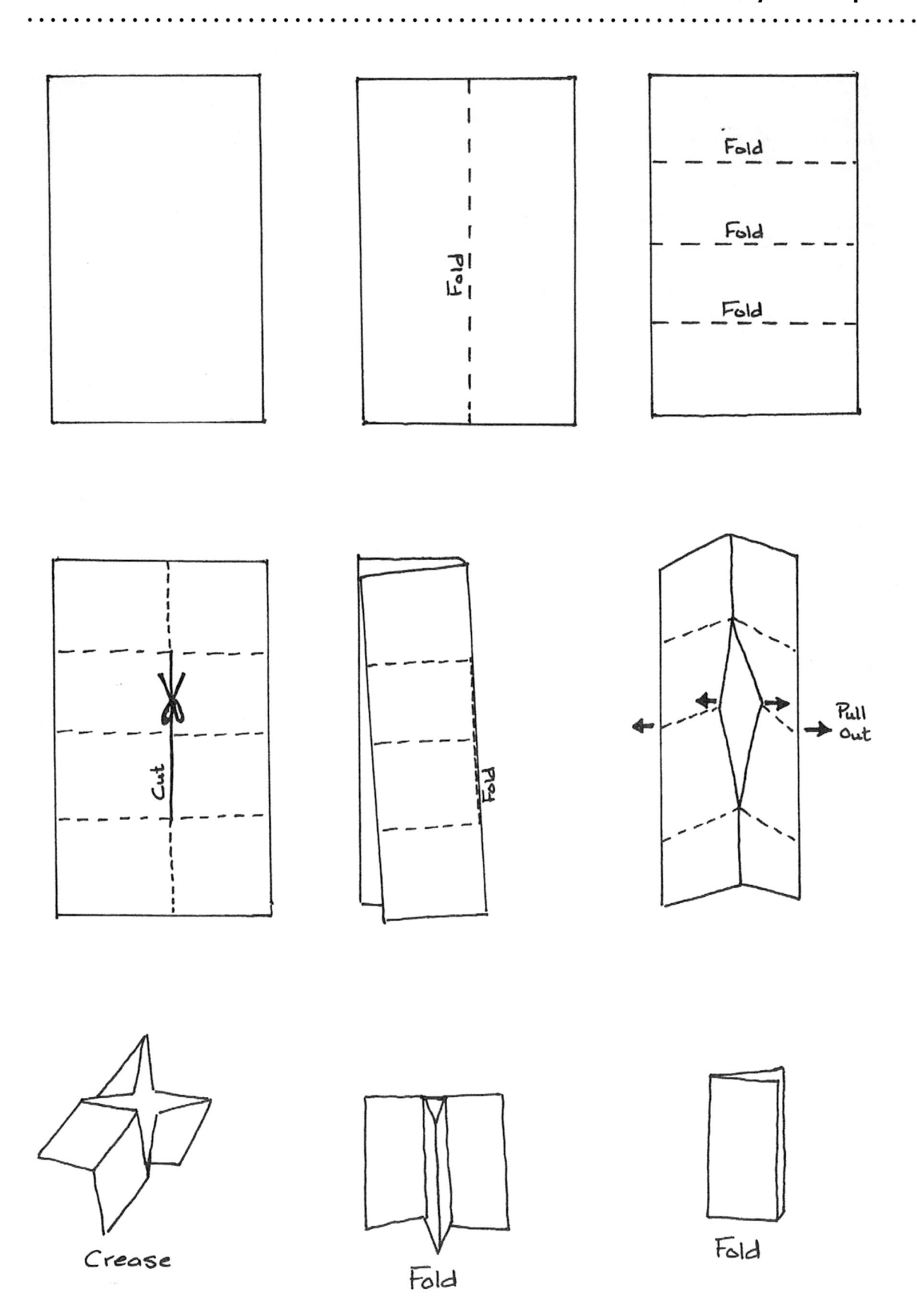

Fold

Fold
Fold
Fold

Cut
Fold

Pull Out

Crease
Fold
Fold

179

Self-efficacy and responsibility

Be your own life coach

SESSION OBJECTIVES

To develop the skills to be your own life coach.

SESSION OUTCOMES

- ✓ A list of positive comments.
- ✓ Understand the importance of feelings, thoughts and behaviour.

LESSON PLAN

- ➢ Remind the children of a time when they observed the parent of their class baby help the baby achieve something – putting a shape in the shape sorter, putting an object in a pot, putting the lid on a pot etc. Discuss how they did this – their tone of voice, the words they used, their belief in the baby's ability.

- ➢ Remind them of how they felt when they observed the baby struggle.

- ➢ Remind them of the stages the baby when through before they succeeded in doing something.

For those classrooms not able to undertake the Circles for Learning Project, video clips or photographs can be used to support the discussion around the topic and stimulate thoughts and ideas from the children and young people.

1. Divide the class into groups. Ask each group to look at the coaching pictures and identify what skills the coach needs to have to help/support/develop/strengthen his team.

2. Imagine that the coaches' comments are like gold coins being put in the bank and that the players' negative comments/thoughts make the gold coins vanish. For the team/player to be successful the bank balance needs to be healthy.

3. Choose one of the pictures and then in groups write on the gold coins some of the comments that the coach might use to build his team/player up and make them feel positive about themselves and their abilities.

Self-efficacy and responsibility

4. Share some of these comments with the other groups.

5. Choose the top 10 comments.

Remind the children and young people about being their own life coach. Help them explore the self-talk they use when doing a task or piece of work.

Remind the children that each time a parent or teacher does a task for us they are stealing our learning opportunity.

Introduce the concept of scaffolding learning – being there to support but not steal the opportunity.

RESOURCES

1. Sticky notes

2. Photographs of coaches working with teams or individuals

3. Thoughts, Feelings, Actions Triangle

4. Gold coins

5. Large piggy bank/pile of gold

IMPORTANT POINTS

- We need to be our own best friend.

- Self-talk is our internal coach.

LEARNING LINKS

Speaking and listening, collaboration, information processing, questioning, observation, creativity, planning and organisation, teamwork.

REFLECTION

Questions:

Positive comment from child:

Self-efficacy and responsibility

Positive comment from adult:

LEARNING DIMENSIONS		SOCIAL & EMOTIONAL SKILLS	
Strategic awareness	🟧	Emotional literacy	🟩
Learning relationships		Neuroscience	
Curiosity	🟧	Self-regulation	
Creativity	🟧	Self-development	🟩
Meaning making	🟧		
Changing & learning	🟧		
Resilience	🟩		

Self-efficacy and responsibility

183

Self-efficacy and responsibility

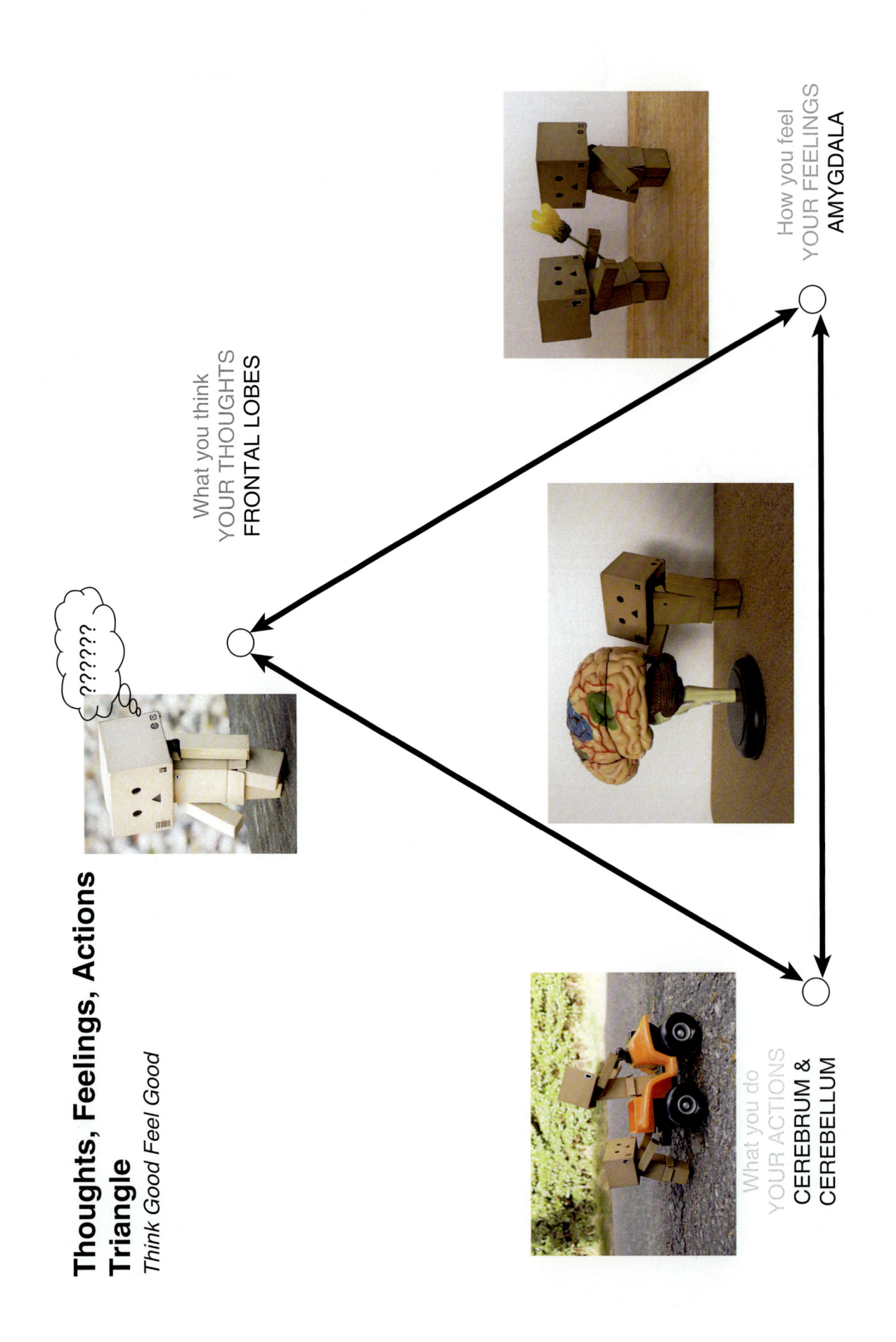

Thoughts, Feelings, Actions Triangle
Think Good Feel Good

What you think
YOUR THOUGHTS
FRONTAL LOBES

How you feel
YOUR FEELINGS
AMYGDALA

What you do
YOUR ACTIONS
CEREBRUM &
CEREBELLUM

184 — Copyright material from Alison Waterhouse (2019), *Self-Discovery*, Routledge

Bibliography

Bowen, R. (2017). *My Incredible Talking Body.* Herndon, VA: Mascot Books.

Calkins, S.D. (1994). 'Origins and outcomes of individual differences in emotional regulation.' In N. A. Fox (ed.), *The Development of Emotional Regulation: Biological and Behavioural Considerations.* Monographs of the Society for Research in Children's Development, 59 (2–3), 53–72.

'**Dr Siegel's hand model of the brain**', https://www.youtube.com/watch?v=f-m2YcdMdFw (accessed 6 November 2018).

Dweck, C. S. (2007). *Mindsets: The New Psychology of Success.* New York: Ballantine Books.

Ferry, B. and Lichtenheld, T. (2015). *Stick and Stone.* Boston, MA: Houghton Mifflin Harcourt.

'**How the amydala hijacks the brain**', https://www.youtube.com/watch?v=xNY0AAUtH3g (accessed 6 November 2018).

Kelly, M. (2009). *Why Am I Here? A Story About Becoming the Best Version of Yourself.* Cincinnati, OH: Beacon Childrens.

Könnecke, O. (2015). *You Can Do It, Bert.* Wellington, New Zealand: Gecko Press.

Kranz, L. (2013). *Only One You.* Boulder, CO: Taylor Trade Publishing.

'**Mirror neurons part 1**', https://www.youtube.com/watch?v=XzMqPYfeA-s (accessed 24 September 2018).

'**Mirror neurons part 2**', https://www.youtube.com/watch?v=xmEsGQ3JmKg (accessed 24 September 2018).

Mischel, W. (2015). *The Marshmallow Test: Understanding Self-Control and How to Master It.* London: Corgi Books.

Neimark, J. and Wong, N. (2015). *The Hugging Tree: A Story about Resilience.* Washington, DC: Magination Press.

Reynolds, P. (2005). *Ish.* London: Walker Books.

'**RSA ANIMATE: The empathic civilisation**', Jeremy Rifkin, https://www.youtube.com/watch?v=l7AWnfFRc7g (accessed 24 September 2018).

Bibliography

Shanker, S. with Barker, T. (2016). *Self-Reg: How to Help Your Child (and You) Break the Stress Cycle and Successfully Engage with Life.* London: Yellow Kite.

Sornson, B. (2013). *Stand in My Shoes: Kids Learning about Empathy.* Golden, CO: Love and Logic Press.

Spires, A. (2017). *The Most Magnificent Thing.* Toronto: Kids Can Press.

Steadman, I. (2013). 'Study: People without brain's "fear centre" can still be scared', *Wired*, February 13, http://www.wired.co.uk/news/archive/2013-02/04/amygdala-brain-fear-centre-mystery (accessed 24 September 2018).

'The visual cliff experiment', https://www.youtube.com/watch?v=p6cqNhHrMJA (accessed 6 November 2018).

Tomlinson, J. (2004). *The Owl Who Was Afraid of the Dark.* London: Egmont.

Ward, H. and Anderson, W. (2013). *The Tin Forest.* London: Templar Publishing.